Shakespeare with Children

Six Scripts for Young Players

Shakespeare with Children
Six Scripts for Young Players

BY Elizabeth Weinstein
ILLUSTRATED BY ANNA DALLAM

A SMITH AND KRAUS BOOK
HANOVER, NEW HAMPSHIRE

A Smith and Kraus Book
Published by Smith and Kraus, Inc.
177 Lyme Road, Hanover, NH 03755
www.smithandkraus.com

First Edition: May 2008
Manufactured in the United States of America
10 9 8 7 6 5 4 3 2 1

Book production by Julia Gignoux, Freedom Hill Design
Text design by Kate Mueller, Electric Dragon Productions
Cover design by A. Shahan; cover art by Anna Dallam

Library of Congress Control Number: 2007939330
ISBN: 978-1-57525-573-6

To my first and best teachers, my parents

Anne Kingsley Thorpe and Donald Weinstein

Contents

Acknowledgments

There are four people without whom this book would not have been written. My husband, Steven Shahan, and our children, Lydia and Nathaniel (my favorite thespians), never once questioned the rightness of this project. And without the example of Vickie Marchand, the idea never would have occurred to me.

For their diverse and wonderful gifts, I say thank you to Leslie Brown, Bill Cross, Anna Dallam, Jennifer Delahunty, Patricia Downes, Libby Ester, Jane Hamilton, Bethany Harris, Annette Hogan, Gary Maggi, Janet Price-Kurta, Marianne Ralbovsky, Laura Reeder, Annie Shahan, Beatrice Susman, Deborah Turner, and Rachel Wysoker.

Introduction

Why Perform Classroom Plays?

If you're holding this book open and reading these words, chances are you have already made the leap into classroom theater with your elementary- or middle-school students. Or you are part of a community youth theater, a home-schooling group, or a summer camp that offers drama. If so, you've already seen how readily children embark on play production. You see the connections between acting and reading, writing, social studies, art, music, even science, as students explore ideas from different times and different worlds.

Perhaps your school district already sponsors periodic field trips to local theaters, brings in professional actors for special performances, or provides videos of stage productions for your students. Attending plays and watching actors perform has a lot of value, and most educators appreciate these cultural offerings. In that case, it should be an easy step to convince your principal or coteachers that rehearsing and performing drama is a profitable way to spend precious classroom hours, disguised as a fun activity.

Having students create their own theatrical performance is entirely different from having them watch it. It is an activity in which every one of your students can participate, under your guidance and by your timetable. It costs virtually nothing and requires no tickets, no special buses, no chaperones, and little if any technology. All students can act, regardless of how proficient their reading is—and it is the rare child who doesn't want to be onstage at least for a few minutes.

Letting children perform in short plays and inviting them to watch their classmates perform focuses their energy and sparks excitement in ways that listening to stories or watching professionals cannot do. Words can unexpectedly come alive for the child who speaks them. A character who is "silly" or "scary" on the page becomes meaningful when a child dresses up and becomes that character herself. A silky polyester blouse that belonged to Grandma, a neighbor's cape from last Halloween, and a pair of big sister's leggings suddenly becomes a costume, and the child wearing that costume walks out and feels the magic.

And Why Shakespeare?

Joy, greed, love, jealousy, sadness, gluttony, fear, playfulness, curiosity, and giddy delight: These are some of the human emotions and conditions reflected in Shakespeare's characters. What child has not felt all of them by a very young age? Trickery and practical joking, murder, celebration, revenge, war, poisoning, madness, and courtship: These are all woven into Shakespeare's dramas, and they fascinate children. Plus, in Shakespeare's plays, these emotions and themes are meant to be acted out—not simply read or passively studied. Most children learn best by doing, and acting lets kids "own" the speech and the rhythm, the humor and the pathos.

By introducing William Shakespeare to elementary-school students, you are giving them a huge gift. Most children have heard the word "Shakespeare"—such is the power of his immortality. If older siblings or friends have attended a Shakespeare play, acted in one, or read one in school, your students will already associate Shakespeare with "the big kids" or with adults. And they will be ready to learn who he was and what he was all about. They will be excited to learn that Shakespeare wrote more varied, complex, and poetic plays than anyone before or since. They will be impressed that Elizabethan theater took the place of television, the Internet, movies, and magazines for thousands of ordinary people. You can emphasize that Shakespeare was a very real person who cared deeply about perfecting his craft.

Working with fourth and fifth graders in my own local school brought me into a new relationship with these plays. I immediately shed the pretensions of a literature student and an educated theatergoer and felt part of a completely absorbing learning experience. Let me put that another way: It was so much fun! My own delight in Shakespeare grew when I watched fourth graders speak his lines and heard them chat confidently offstage about the dilemmas of his characters Lysander and Hermia, Puck, Romeo, and Lady Macbeth.

Producing Shakespeare with children, we learn or relearn what the plays are about and what their purpose is, namely to remind us of our history and our common humanity, to instruct, and to entertain—all at the same time.

Practical Matters

How long will it take you to produce one of these plays? It depends. If you are in a school setting and have a half-hour to forty-five-minute reading period once a day, then you will probably need at least three weeks. Count in time for reading aloud a story version of the play, learning some background, and reading the script aloud as a group before the play is cast. If you have longer stretches in which to rehearse, you may be able to produce the play in less time, but most children can't rehearse for hours on end.

I have called these productions "classroom theater" because I hope educators realize that a formal stage is not a requirement. (Some teachers may not even stage them at all, but might assign parts and use the script as a read-aloud exercise in class.) Of course it is nice to have the option of using an auditorium, gym, or cafeteria, but you can rehearse them—and even perform them—in a classroom or outside on the playground.

Stage directions should be as simple as you can make them, and children will ignore many of your suggestions. That's all right. Your goal should be to get them to come forward and say their lines clearly and with emotion and to relate to the other characters in the scene. With some groups the biggest issue is volume. The easiest way to deal with the problem of inaudible lines is to ask those children who aren't acting in a particular scene to watch their fellow performers from the back of the room. If they can't hear, an audience won't be able to hear either.

Shakespeare is in the public domain, so we can edit his work without receiving permission. I have substantially adapted these plays, and they are best suited for children up to the age of about twelve. But while I have shortened speeches and cut out whole scenes and characters, I've tried hard to keep the lines spoken by your students pure Shakespeare. That is, the words spoken trippingly on their tongues are the ones the Bard himself wrote. There just are not as many of them.

The narrator is the link between the audience and the action onstage. In one production I assisted, we had a different narrator for each act of the play, and the new narrator entered and announced, "Act I" or "Act II." (Note that any role can be double-cast, not just the narrator—that is, assigned to more than one child.)

While the characters rarely have more than five lines to speak at a time, the narrators may have more because they can read their parts. The narrators move the plot along by announcing action that will take place or by summing up what has just taken place—in case the audience misses something. They are vital, and it's important to give these parts to able readers with strong voices.

There are music, set, prop, and costume suggestions included, but feel free to do things your way. Music is an invaluable addition to these plays. Shakespeare incorporated music freely, and productions of his comedies and romances always included dance as well. Use student musicians to play a tune—any tune—at intervals or between acts. If this isn't possible, recorded music will also add depth and beauty to your performance. The music I've cited is generally period music (Renaissance) or music with a period sound. Feel free to be creative in your choices. You will be in good company if you experiment with rock, folk, pop, or classical music for your production.

A painted backdrop or two—castle, forest, battlefield—is wonderful, and some children prefer behind-the-scenes work. Backdrops aren't essential, but many children find it easier to grasp a different place and time when there is visual evidence. Scenery can be reused for years if it is fairly generic.

Costumes can be as simple as T-shirts, scarves, nightgowns, and leggings. Check out thrift stores, backs of closets, and friends' attics. Please don't allow one or two diligent parents to sew costumes for everyone. It simply is not necessary.

One last thing: I urge you, if you can possibly take the time, to read the original play yourself and share with your students some of what you learned. Yes, your goal is to produce a simple production with children. But reading the original play and referring to some of the helpful notes and definitions included in any decent text will give you a much more solid background, and it will increase your confidence as the play's director.

A Midsummer Night's Dream

Puck, the woodland spirit. *Puck's costume leaves ample room for self-expression. This one combines a headpiece of leaves, a simple tunic, and a silky scarf to suggest a character who inhabits a world more fanciful than real.*

With its blend of fantasy and reality, fairies and mortals, conflict and happy resolution, the comedy *A Midsummer Night's Dream* offers children a rich introduction to Shakespeare. It is probably the most popular of Shakespeare's plays, and the one that children are most likely to have heard of or to have seen. It was written in 1595 or 1596, representing the transition from Shakespeare's early lighter comedies to his more mature plays.

What will grade-school students like about this play?

Even though the play isn't always easy to follow, there are several elements that really appeal to children:

- Four young people—two pairs of lovers—get into a seemingly hopeless tangle that comes right in the end.

- The fairy character Puck (or Robin Goodfellow) flits about, administering magic potions and ointments that cause people to do and say things they wouldn't otherwise do or say.

- Fairies with fanciful names (Peaseblossom and Mustardseed) dance and sing and trick each other. There are many opportunities for music and dance in this play, though it can also be performed simply and with background music alone.

- The character Bottom is pompous, gets a lot of words wrong, and is tricked into wearing a donkey's head.

- The fairy queen Titania is tricked by Puck into falling in love with Bottom when he is wearing the donkey head.

As in all the scripts in this book, the play's events are regularly forecast and summarized by the narrator. So even though there are four plot lines, most children will be able to keep them straight if they listen to the narrators.

The play is set in ancient Athens and opens in the palace of Duke Theseus. The duke announces that in four days he will marry Hippolyta, Queen of the Amazons. The first plot deals with Duke Theseus's plans for involving the whole city of Athens in a great celebration.

The second plot involves two pairs of young lovers. A young woman named Hermia wants to marry a young man named Lysander, and he wants to marry her. But Hermia's father insists that she marry another man—Demetrius—whom she does not love, or face the consequences. By Athenian law, Hermia's father may have her put to death for refusing to marry Demetrius, and he seeks the duke's support in threatening her with that punishment. Hermia and Lysander decide to run away. Before they do, they confide their plans to Hermia's best friend, Helena—who, as it turns out, is in love with Demetrius. Unfortunately, Demetrius doesn't love Helena. He loves Hermia and insists on his right to marry her.

A third plot involves the exploits of a band of merry Athenian laborers who gather in the forest to rehearse a play in honor of the duke's nuptials. The headiness of a long night causes an unexpected twist in which one of these players gets tangled up in the fairy world that exists deep in the woods. And the fourth plot moves us further into that realm with another royal couple: the jealous Oberon, King of the Fairies, and his beautiful and proud Queen Titania.

A Midsummer Night's Dream interweaves the two settings of the real world and the fairy world so smoothly that by the end, the characters have the sense that they have been asleep and dreaming. The play is not all silliness and trickiness, but even young actors know that we mortals can be foolish and wrong. Seeing the real characters and the fairies mirror each other's imperfections can be simple fun for the youngest children and a more complex adventure for older ones.

Suggested Music

Songs & Dances from Shakespeare (compact disc). The Broadside Band, Saydisc Records, 1994.

Come, Gentle Night: Music of Shakespeare's World (compact disc). Ensemble Galilei, Telarc Records, 2000.

Other suggestions for live or recorded music: any Renaissance dance music or simple tunes played on the recorder, flute, guitar, or instrument of your choice.

Suggested Props

Paper (for the players' play scripts)

Flower

Fruit

Cardboard painted to look like the character "Wall"

Suggested Backdrops

Grand palace

Forest

Backdrop note: If you have a curtain and you want to stage a realistic production, consider making the forest scenes the main backdrop. All other scenes could then be staged in front of the curtain.

Suggested Costumes

The human characters should be dressed as follows: belted tunics (blouses or shirts) for the men and long dresses for the women. The duke should be somewhat grander than the other men, and Hippolyta somewhat more elegant than the young women. The forest fairies can wear any combination of scarves or capes to help create an ethereal image. Let your imagination be your guide in dressing Puck, whether the character is played by a girl or a boy. Puck can be sweet and fairylike or he or she can look somewhat more sinister. Make your donkey head as large and obvious as possible: The scenes where Titania is kissing and cooing over the donkey head will be humorous. Make a head out of papier-mâché or a hood out of cloth, or invest in a large rubber or plastic mask.

Cast of Characters

Narrator(s)

The four young lovers

> Hermia
>
> Lysander
>
> Helena
>
> Demetrius

Casting note: Because the four young lovers are so similar, it can be hard for audiences to tell Hermia and Lysander from Helena and Demetrius. Consider using an obvious physical characteristic such as hair color or height to identify each couple. Or one couple could wear white or light costumes and the other a dark color. In the original play, there are references to Hermia being short and Helena being tall (Act III, Scene 2).

The palace

> Duke Theseus, Duke of Athens
>
> Hippolyta, Queen of the Amazons and Duke Theseus's betrothed
>
> Egeus, father of Hermia
>
> Philostrate, master of revels in Duke Theseus's court

The players

> Nick Bottom, the weaver
>
> Peter Quince, the carpenter
>
> Francis Flute, the bellows-mender
>
> Tom Snout, the tinker

Snug, the joiner (carpenter)

Robin Starveling, the tailor

The fairies in the wood

Oberon, King of the fairies

Titania, Queen of the fairies

Puck (also called Robin Goodfellow in the original),
    a hobgoblin who serves Oberon

Fairy, servant to Titania

Peaseblossom, fairy attending Titania

Cobweb, fairy attending Titania

Mote, fairy attending Titania

Mustardseed, fairy attending Titania

Pronunciation Guide to Names

Demetrius (di-mee-tree-uhs)

Egeus (ee-gee-uhs)

Helena (hel-uh-nuh)

Hermia (her-mee-uh)

Hippolyta (hih-pol-ih-tuh)

Lysander (lie-san-der)

Oberon (oh-buh-ron)

Philostrate (feel-oh-stra-tay)

Pyramus (peer-uh-muss)

Theseus (thee-see-uhs)

Thisbe (thiz-bee)

Titania (tie-tay-nee-uh)

Scenes

The court of Duke Theseus and the woods.

A Midsummer Night's Dream

ACT I
Scene 1

Duke's palace.

(Horn sounds. ENTER NARRATOR, DUKE THESEUS, HIPPOLYTA, EGEUS, PHILOSTRATE, HERMIA, LYSANDER, and DEMETRIUS.)

(These characters strike statuelike poses as Narrator speaks: Duke and Hippolyta hand in hand, with Egeus and Demetrius opposite them and the other two young people behind them.)

NARRATOR:

Love is grand, when it goes smoothly—when the person you love loves you back and when everyone you care about approves of the person you love. Then everything is right with the world, and you can get married and live happily ever after. But even in Mr. William Shakespeare's time, and even before that—in ancient Athens, where Shakespeare set this play—love didn't always run smoothly. Why should it? That's life!

You see before you the court of Duke Theseus, the Duke of Athens, in Greece. The duke is a lucky man, because after he captured Hippolyta, Queen of the Amazons, he fell in love with her, and she fell in love with him too and has agreed to marry him in four days.

But meanwhile an old man, Egeus, has troubles. His daughter Hermia and a young man named Lysander want to get married, but long ago Egeus decided that his daughter would marry a man named Demetrius. Hermia refuses to marry Demetrius. Now, in ancient Athens, it was the rule that when children refused to marry the people their parents wanted them to marry, their parents could have them put to death. Egeus has come before Duke Theseus to say that if his daughter continues to refuse marriage to Demetrius, he requests permission to have her put to death.

This play is a comedy! Welcome!

(As Narrator finishes speech, characters start to move.)

DUKE THESEUS:

Now, fair Hippolyta, our nuptial hour

Draws on apace. Four happy days bring in
Another moon. But O, methinks how slow
This old moon wanes!

HIPPOLYTA:

Four days will quickly steep themselves in night, my love.
Four nights will quickly dream away the time.

DUKE THESEUS:

Go, Philostrate,
Stir up the Athenian youth and have them make merriment
For our wedding day.

PHILOSTRATE:

Yes, my lord.

(He bows and EXITS.)

DUKE THESEUS:

(Turning to Egeus.)
Egeus, good man, what's the news with thee?

EGEUS:

Full of vexation come I, with complaint
Against my child, my daughter Hermia.
Stand forth, Demetrius. —My noble lord,
This man hath my consent to marry Hermia.
Stand forth, Lysander. —And, my gracious duke,
This man *(Gestures to Lysander.)* hath bewitched my child
With rhymes and love tokens and songs.
Sir, you have turned her obedience to me
Into stubborn harshness.
I therefore beg the ancient privilege of Athens:
Either she shall have this gentleman Demetrius
Or, according to our law, she shall go to her death.

DUKE THESEUS:

What say you, Hermia? Demetrius is a worthy gentleman.

HERMIA:

So is Lysander.
I do beg your Grace to pardon me.
May I know the worst that will befall me
If I refuse to wed Demetrius?

DUKE THESEUS:

> Either to die or give up forever
> The society of men
> And live as a nun in a shady cloister all your life,
> Chanting faint hymns to the cold, fruitless moon.

DEMETRIUS:

> Relent, sweet Hermia!
> Lysander, give up your claim to what is mine.

LYSANDER:

> You have her father's love, Demetrius.
> Let me have Hermia's. Do you marry him!

EGEUS:

> Scornful Lysander.
> She is mine, and all my right of her
> I give to Demetrius.

DUKE THESEUS:

> Come, Egeus and Demetrius, I must
> Employ in some business
> For our upcoming wedding.
> Hermia, look you prepare yourself and
> Think of what you will do. —Come, Hippolyta, my love.

(EXIT DUKE THESEUS, HIPPOLYTA, DEMETRIUS, and EGEUS.)

LYSANDER:

> How now, my love? Why is your cheek so pale?
> The course of true love never did run smooth.

HERMIA:

> Yes, true lovers have ever been crossed.
> Let us teach our trial patience.

LYSANDER:

> Gentle Hermia, hear me. Flee thy father's house tomorrow night . . .

(Lysander and Hermia move back and confer in private conversation as Narrator speaks.)

NARRATOR:

> Lysander persuades his beloved Hermia to leave her father's house and go through the woods to a place outside Athens where the harsh laws will no

longer affect them. He will leave first and meet her in the woods. As the two of them discuss this plan, Hermia's dear friend Helena enters. Just to complicate things, it happens that Helena is in love with Demetrius. She knows Hermia is supposed to marry him and she is jealous.

(ENTER HELENA.)

HERMIA:

Godspeed, fair Helena, my friend.

HELENA:

Fair? Call you me fair?
Alas, Demetrius loves YOUR fair.
My ear should catch your voice, my eye your eye;
My tongue should catch your tongue's sweet melody.
O Hermia—teach me how you look and with what art
You sway the motion of Demetrius's heart!

HERMIA:

I frown upon him, yet he loves me still.

HELENA:

O, if your frowns could teach my smiles.

HERMIA:

I give him curses, yet he gives me love.
The more I hate, the more he follows me.

HELENA:

The more I love, the more he hateth me.

HERMIA:

Helena, old friend. Take comfort.
Demetrius no more shall see my face.
Lysander and I will fly this place.

LYSANDER:

Helena, to you our minds we will unfold.

(The three of them sit down while Lysander tells Helena the plan.)

NARRATOR:

Lysander and Hermia are eager to tell Helena what they're about to do. Hermia tells Helena that in the woods where they used to play together, that is where she and Lysander intend to meet and leave Athens behind. Helena decides to find Demetrius and tell him about Hermia and Lysander's plan.

She realizes that although Demetrius may thank her for giving him this information, doing so won't make him love her instead of Hermia. But she can't resist, and off she goes to find him.

(The characters stand up. HERMIA and LYSANDER clasp hands, then EXIT. HELENA EXITS.)

ACT I
Scene 2

The woods.

(ENTER QUINCE, SNUG, BOTTOM, FLUTE, SNOUT, and STARVELING as Narrator speaks.)

NARRATOR:

In the palace woods, all is not quiet or especially peaceful. A group of Athenian laborers led by their friend Quince the carpenter have decided to put on a little play and perform it at Duke Theseus's wedding. Quince has gathered them in the wood for a rehearsal.

QUINCE:

Is all our company here? Here is our play for the duke and duchess on their wedding day.

BOTTOM:

First, good Peter Quince, say what the play treats on, then read the names of the actors and go to the point.

QUINCE:

Marry, our play is "The Most Lamentable Comedy and Most Cruel Death of Pyramus and Thisbe." You, Nick Bottom, you are Pyramus.

BOTTOM:

Is Pyramus a lover or a tyrant?

QUINCE:

A lover who kills himself for love. Now, Francis Flute—you must be Thisbe, the lady that Pyramus must love.

FLUTE:

Nay, let me not play a woman! I have a beard coming.

BOTTOM:

I could play Thisbe too. I'll speak in a monstrous little voice. *(Speaking in a shrill voice.)* "Thisbe! Thisbe!"

QUINCE:

No, no, you must play Pyramus. —Robin Starveling, the tailor?

STARVELING:

Here, Peter Quince.

QUINCE:

You must play Thisbe's mother. —Tom Snout, the tinker?

SNOUT:

Here, Peter Quince.

QUINCE:

You must play Pyramus's father. Myself, Thisbe's father. Snug, the joiner, you have the lion's part. And there I hope is a play well fitted.

SNUG:

Have you the lion's part already written? If you do, give it to me, for I am slow of study.

QUINCE:

It is nothing but roaring.

BOTTOM:

Let me play the lion too. I will roar to do any man's heart good. The duke will say "Let him roar again. Let him roar again!"

QUINCE:

If you did it terribly, you would frighten the duchess and all the ladies and they would hang us all.

ALL IN UNISON (except for Bottom):

They would hang us, every mother's son!

BOTTOM:

But I would roar gently . . .

QUINCE:

You can play no part but Pyramus. *(Getting exasperated.)* You must play Pyramus!

BOTTOM:

Well, I will undertake it.

QUINCE:

Now, masters, here are your parts for you to learn. Meet me to rehearse tomorrow night by moonlight in the palace wood.

(EXIT ALL.)

ACT II
Scene 1

(ENTER FAIRY from one side of stage and PUCK from other.)

PUCK:

How now, Spirit, whither wander you?

FAIRY:

Over hill, over dale,
Through bush, through brier
Over park, over pale
Through flood, through fire.
I do wander everywhere
Swifter than the moon's sphere.
I serve the Fairy Queen
To dew her orbs upon the green.

PUCK:

The king doth keep his revels here tonight.
Take care the queen comes not within his sight!

FAIRY:

Either I mistake your shape and making quite,
Or else you are Puck, that shrewd and knavish sprite.

PUCK:

I am Puck, that merry wanderer of the night.
I jest to Oberon and make him smile—
But make room, fairy. Here comes Oberon.

FAIRY:

And here my mistress.

(FAIRY and PUCK EXIT while Narrator speaks.)

NARRATOR:

There is a world inhabited by spirits and fairies deep within the wood. You just saw Puck, a hobgoblin who serves Oberon, King of the fairies, talking to a fairy who serves Titania, Queen of the fairies. At the moment King Oberon and Queen Titania are quarreling. Titania has adopted a little Indian boy and she dotes on him, which has made Oberon very jealous.

(ENTER OBERON, PUCK, and TITANIA with her FAIRIES.)

OBERON:

Ill met by moonlight, proud Titania.

TITANIA:

What, jealous Oberon?

OBERON:

Am not I thy lord?

TITANIA:

Then I must be thy lady.

But these be the forgeries of thy jealousy

And with your brawls you have disturbed our sport.

The ox has stretched his yoke in vain.

The plowman has lost his sweat,

And the green corn is rotted before its time.

The spring, the summer, the fruitful autumn and angry winter

Change their usual outfits and we know not which is which.

All these evils and many more come from our quarrel.

We are their parents and their original.

OBERON:

Do you then repair the quarrel. It lies within your power.

Why should Titania cross her Oberon?

I do but beg your little changeling boy

To be my squire.

TITANIA:

No! Set your heart at rest.

His mother vowed to serve me.

Full often hath she gossiped by my side

And sat with me on Neptune's yellow sands.

But she was mortal and did die

And for her I do rear up her boy

And for her I will not part with him.

OBERON:

How long within this wood intend you to stay?

TITANIA:

Perchance till after Duke Theseus's wedding day.

Go with us and dance in our round and see our moonlight revels.

OBERON:

Give me that boy and I will go with thee.

TITANIA:

Not for thy fairy kingdom.
(To the fairy or fairies.) Away! We shall fight downright
If I longer stay.

(EXIT TITANIA with FAIRY or FAIRIES.)

OBERON:

My gentle Puck, come hither.

(PUCK ENTERS.)

OBERON:

Fetch me that little western flower where once fell Cupid's fiery shaft—
the maidens call it "love-in-idleness." Fetch me that flower.

PUCK:

(Starting to skip and dance.) I'll put a girdle round the earth
in forty minutes.

(EXIT PUCK.)

OBERON:

I'll watch Titania when she is asleep
And drop the flower's juice in her eyes.
The next thing she sees when she does awake—
Be it lion, bear, or wolf, or bull
Be it meddling monkey or busy ape—
She shall pursue it with the soul of love.
. . . But who comes here?
I will be invisible.

(Oberon hides. ENTER DEMETRIUS followed by HELENA.)

DEMETRIUS:

I love thee not. Therefore, pursue me not.
Where is Lysander and fair Hermia?
You told me they fled into this wood,
And here am I.
Get thee gone, and follow me no more.

HELENA:

You draw me, you hard-hearted magnet.

DEMETRIUS:

Do I not in plainest truth
Tell you I do not, I cannot, love you?

HELENA:

And even for that, I love you the more.

DEMETRIUS:

Do not tempt the hatred of my spirit.
For I am sick when I do look on thee.

HELENA:

And I am sick when I look NOT on you.

DEMETRIUS:

Where is your modesty? I'll run from thee
And leave thee to the mercy of wild beasts.

(EXIT DEMETRIUS, angrily.)

HELENA:

The wildest hath not such a heart as you.
I'll follow thee.

(EXIT HELENA, following him.)

(ENTER PUCK. Oberon comes out from hiding. Puck gives him the flower.)

OBERON:

Pray, give me the flower—
With the juice of this I'll charm my Queen Titania's eyes.
You too, take some of it and seek through this grove
A sweet Athenian lady who is in love
With a disdainful youth.

(Oberon pulls Puck aside and gives him part of the flower, whispering in his ear.)

NARRATOR:

Oberon has been watching Helena and Demetrius with great interest. He sees that the human world has just as many problems as the fairy world, and he decides to interfere. He tells Puck to put the magic flower juice in Demetrius's eyes as well—he will make Demetrius love Helena when he wakes up.

OBERON:

> Anoint his eyes also
> So that the next thing he sees will be this lady.

PUCK:

> Fear not, my lord. Your servant Puck shall do this.

(EXIT PUCK and OBERON.)

ACT II
Scene 2

(ENTER TITANIA and FAIRIES.)

(MUSIC.)

TITANIA:

> Come now a roundel and a fairy song
> Sing me now asleep.
> Then to your fairy business and let me rest.

FIRST FAIRY:

> You spotted snakes with double tongue
> Thorny hedgehogs, be not seen.
> Newts and blindworms, do no wrong,
> Come not near our Fairy Queen.

FAIRY CHORUS:

> Lulla, lulla, lullaby, lulla, lulla, lullaby.
> Nor spell nor charm.
> Come our lovely lady nigh.
> So good night, with lullaby.

SECOND FAIRY:

> Hence, away! Now all is well.
> One aloof stand sentinel.

(EXIT FAIRIES.)

(ENTER OBERON, who squeezes the flower over Titania's eyelids.)

OBERON:

> What thou seest when thou dost wake,
> Do it for thy true love take.
> When thou waks't, it is thy dear.

Wake when some vile thing is near!

(EXIT OBERON.)

(ENTER LYSANDER and HERMIA.)

LYSANDER:

Fair love, you faint with wand'ring in the wood.
And to speak truth, I have forgot our way.

HERMIA:

Be it so, Lysander. Find you out a bed,
For I upon this bank will rest my head.

*(The two of them arrange themselves some distance apart and
lie down to sleep.)*

NARRATOR:

Lysander and Hermia have wandered through the woods and have gotten off course in the dark. Now they decide to rest and continue later. Whether or not this is a good idea, you shall soon see. When Puck enters this resting spot and sees the two lovers, he assumes that they are the young Athenian couple Oberon was talking about. And Oberon has instructed him to give the young man the same treatment Titania has received. When awaking, Lysander will love the first thing he sees.

*(ENTER PUCK. He spies Lysander and goes over to him, squeezes the
flower over Lysander's eyes. EXITS.)*

(ENTER DEMETRIUS and HELENA, running.)

HELENA:

Stay, sweet Demetrius. Wilt thou leave me in the dark?

DEMETRIUS:

Stay, on thy peril. I alone will go.

(EXIT DEMETRIUS.)

HELENA:

O, I am out of breath in this fond chase.
The more my prayer, the lesser is my grace.
(Sees Lysander.) But who is here? Lysander, on the ground!
Lysander, if you live, good sir, awake.

(Lysander wakes, stands, and stretches.)

LYSANDER:

And run through fire I will for thy sake.
O Helena! Where is Demetrius?
O, how fit a word
Is that vile name to perish on my sword!

HELENA:

Do not say so. Lysander, say not so.
Because Demetrius loves your Hermia?
Hermia loves you, so be content.

LYSANDER:

Content with Hermia? No, I do regret
The tedious hours with her I've spent.
Not Hermia, but Helena I love.
Who will not change a raven for a dove?

HELENA:

To what do I owe this mockery?
Wherefore do I deserve this scorn?

(EXIT HELENA.)

LYSANDER:

Hermia, sleep thou there.
And never come Lysander near.
Now I address all my powers and all my might
To honor Helena and to be her knight.

(EXIT LYSANDER.)

(Hermia wakes.)

HERMIA:

Help me, Lysander, help me!
What a dream was here!
Lysander, look how I do quake with fear.
Methought a serpent ate my heart away,
And you sat smiling at his cruel prey.
Lysander? Lysander, my lord!
What, out of hearing? Gone? No sound, no word?

(EXIT HERMIA.)

ACT III
Scene 1

(TITANIA is still asleep on the stage. BOTTOM, QUINCE, and other play-ers ENTER to rehearse. They should be holding scripts in their hands and are milling around in disorganized fashion.)

QUINCE:

Here's a marvelous convenient place for our rehearsal.
This green plot shall be our stage—

BOTTOM:

Peter Quince?

QUINCE:

What, Bottom?

BOTTOM:

There are things in this comedy that will never please. You must write a prologue to say we will do no harm with our swords.

SNOUT:

Will not the ladies be afeared of the lion? We must tell that he is really not a lion.

QUINCE:

We must have moonlight in the chamber. One of you shall play Moonlight. Aye, and another thing—we must have a wall, for Pyramus and Thisbe did talk through a chink in the wall.

BOTTOM:

Some man or other must represent Wall.

(ENTER PUCK, invisible to the others. They keep "rehearsing" as PUCK comes forward to speak to the audience.)

PUCK:

What hempen homespuns have we swaggering here?
I'll be a listener to their play—and perhaps if I see cause,
I may be an actor too.

BOTTOM:

O my dearest Thisbe. Stay thou but here awhile
And by and by I will to thee appear . . .

(EXIT BOTTOM.)

(After BOTTOM speaks his lines and walks offstage, PUCK follows him, mischievously.)

NARRATOR:

The fairies know that they can have fun with mere mortals.
Puck decides to play a joke on Bottom.

(ENTER BOTTOM, wearing a donkey's head or mask. The other players scream.)

QUINCE:

O monstrous! O strange! We are haunted. Pray, masters, fly, masters!
Help!

(QUINCE and the other players RUN OFFSTAGE.)

BOTTOM:

Why do they run away?

(ENTER SNOUT.)

SNOUT:

O Bottom, thou art changed! What do I see on thee?

BOTTOM:

What do you see? Some knavery of your own!

(SNOUT EXITS.)

BOTTOM:

Never mind. I will not stir from this place.
I see their foolish plan, to fright me if they could.

(MUSIC: Bottom can sing, as in original play, or recite.)

The finch, the sparrow, and the lark,
The plainsong cuckoo gray,
Whose note full many a man doth mark
And dares not answer nay . . .

(Bottom struts around and brays like a donkey.)

TITANIA:

(Waking up.) What angel wakes me from my flow'ry bed?
I pray thee, gentle mortal, sing!
On the first view of thee, I love thee.

BOTTOM:

Methinks, mistress, you should have little reason for that. And yet, to say the truth, reason and love keep little company together nowadays.

TITANIA:

Thou art as wise as thou art beautiful. I do love thee.

Come—I'll give thee fairies to attend thee.

They will give thee jewels and sing to thee.

Peaseblossom, Cobweb, Mote, and Mustardseed!

(ENTER four or fewer FAIRIES.)

PEASEBLOSSOM:

Ready.

COBWEB:

And I.

MOTE:

And I.

MUSTARDSEED:

And I.

ALL TOGETHER:

Hail mortal! Where shall we go?

TITANIA:

Wait upon him. Lead him to my bower.

Feed him with apricots and dewberries,

With purple grapes, green figs, and mulberries.

(EXIT TITANIA, BOTTOM, and FAIRIES.)

ACT III
Scene 2

NARRATOR:

In this scene, Oberon is eager to hear from Puck how his trick on Titania has played out. Puck describes how he crept up to Titania as she was sleeping and anointed her with the magic potion that would make her love the first thing she saw. Then he describes seeing the laborers Quince and his friends rehearsing their play in the woods. He decides to have fun with Bottom, making both him and Titania look foolish.

(ENTER OBERON and PUCK.)

PUCK:

And so, Master, my mistress with a monster is in love.

OBERON:

Mad spirit, this has fallen out better than I could devise!
And have you also caught the young Athenian man as I bid thee?

PUCK:

That is finished too—

(ENTER DEMETRIUS and HERMIA. Oberon and Puck step aside so they can't be seen.)

OBERON:

Stand close. This is the same Athenian. But not the woman.

PUCK:

This is the woman. But not this the man!

HERMIA:

If thou hast slain Lysander in his sleep
Kill me too.
Why would he have stolen away
From sleeping Hermia?
It cannot be but thou hast murdered him.

DEMETRIUS:

You pierce me through the heart with your stern cruelty.

HERMIA:

Where is Lysander? Wilt thou give him to me?

DEMETRIUS:

I'd as soon give his carcass to my hounds!

HERMIA:

Out, dog! Out, cur! You try my maiden's patience.
Tell true, even for my sake! Have you slain him sleeping?

DEMETRIUS:

I am not guilty of Lysander's blood,
Nor is he dead, for all I can tell.

HERMIA:

I pray thee, tell me then that he is well.

DEMETRIUS:

And if I could, what should I get then?

HERMIA:

A privilege never to see me more.

(EXIT HERMIA.)

DEMETRIUS:

There is no following her in this vein.
Here, therefore, for a while I will remain.

(DEMETRIUS lies down, falls asleep.)

OBERON:

(To Puck.) What hast thou done?
Quickly! About the wood go swifter than the wind,
And Helena of Athens find.
All fancy—sick she is and pale of cheer.
See thou bring her here.
I'll charm this Demetrius before she does appear.

PUCK:

I go, I go, look how I go.

(EXIT PUCK.)

(Oberon applies the flower potion to Demetrius's eyes.)

(HELENA and LYSANDER ENTER, followed by PUCK.)

PUCK:

Captain of our fairy band,
Helena is here at hand,
And the youth, mistook by me.
Shall we their fond pageant see?
Lord, what fools these mortals be!

LYSANDER:

Why should you think I woo in scorn, dear Helena?

HELENA:

O devilish holy fray!
Your vows are Hermia's. Will you give her over?

LYSANDER:

I had no judgment when to her I swore.
Demetrius loves her, and he loves not you.

DEMETRIUS:

(Waking up.) O Helena! Goddess, nymph, perfect, divine!
O, let me kiss your hand!

HELENA:

O spite! O curses! I see you all are bent
To set against me for your merriment.
Are you both joined to mock me?

LYSANDER:

You are unkind, Demetrius. Be not so,
For you love Hermia, this you know I know.

DEMETRIUS:

Lysander, keep thy Hermia. I will none.
But look where thy love comes. Yonder is thy dear.

(ENTER HERMIA.)

HERMIA:

Mine ear has brought me to thy sound.
Why did you leave me so?

LYSANDER:

Why should I stay when love pressed me to go?

HERMIA:

But what love could press Lysander from my side?

LYSANDER:

My love for fair Helena. Why seek'st thou me?
Could not this make you know
The hate I bear you made me leave you so?

(Silence for a moment.)

HERMIA:

(Wonderingly.) You speak not as you think. It cannot be.

HELENA:

Lo, she is one of them.
Now I perceive they have joined all three
To fashion this false sport in spite of me.
(To Hermia.) Hermia, most ungrateful maid!
What of our schooldays' friendship, our childhood innocence?

So we grew together, and now will you tear our love apart?
Will you join with men in scorning your poor friend?

HERMIA:

I am amazed at your words.
I scorn you not. It seems that you scorn me.

HELENA:

Ay, carry on. Pretend sad looks and
Make faces at me when I turn my back.
Wink at each other, hold the sweet jest up.

LYSANDER:

My love, my life, my soul, fair Helena.

HELENA:

(Sarcastically.) O, excellent!

HERMIA:

(To Lysander.) Sweet, do not scorn her so.

LYSANDER:

Helena, I love thee. By my life, I do.
(To Hermia.) Hang off, thou cat, thou burr! Vile thing, let loose,
Or I will shake thee from me like a serpent.
Be certain, nothing truer, 'tis no jest
That I do hate thee and love Helena.

HERMIA:

O me! *(To Helena.)* You juggler, you cankerblossom,
You thief of love! Have you come by night
And stolen my love's heart from him?

HELENA:

Have you no modesty, no maiden shame?
Fie, fie, you puppet, you!

HERMIA:

Puppet? Why so? Ay, that way goes the game.
With her tall personage, her height,
Forsooth, she hath won my Lysander!
Well, how low am I, thou painted maypole? Speak!
I am not so low that my nails cannot reach your eyes.

HELENA:

Gentlemen, I pray you, though you mock me
Let her not hurt me.
Good Hermia, do not be so bitter with me.
I never wronged you.
And now to Athens will I bear my folly back
And follow you no further. Let me go.

HERMIA:

Get you gone! What hinders you?

HELENA:

A foolish heart I leave here behind—with Demetrius.

LYSANDER:

Be not afraid. She shall not harm you, Helena.

HELENA:

Though she be but little, she is fierce.

HERMIA:

"Little" again? Nothing but "low" and "little"?
Let me at her— *(Rushes toward Helena as if to fight.)*

LYSANDER:

Get you gone, you dwarf, you bead, you acorn!

DEMETRIUS:

You are too eager on Helena's behalf, who scorns your services.
Let her alone. Speak not her part.

LYSANDER:

Now follow and try whose right,
Thine or mine, is most in Helena.

DEMETRIUS:

I'll not follow. Nay, I'll go with thee, cheek by jowl.

(EXIT DEMETRIUS and LYSANDER.)

HELENA:

(To Hermia.) Your hands than mine are quicker for a fray.
My legs are longer, though, to run away.

(EXIT HELENA.)

HERMIA:

I am amazed and know not what to say.

(EXIT HERMIA.)

OBERON:

(To Puck.) This is your mistake—
Unless you did this all purposefully?

PUCK:

Believe me, King of Shadows, I mistook.
Did not you tell me I should know the man
By the Athenian garments he had on?
Still, all this quarreling is great good sport.

OBERON:

The lovers Demetrius and Lysander
Look for a place to fight.
So with stars and fog lead these testy rivals so astray
They will not come within each other's way.
Crush this herb into Lysander's eye
So when he awakes all this will seem a dream
And back to Athens shall the lovers wend
Their union till death shall never end.

(OBERON hands PUCK some more of the magic flower and then EXITS.)

NARRATOR:

While Puck has been enjoying the spectacle of the quarreling lovers, Oberon regrets the mistake and is also more concerned with his own problems. While Puck leads Demetrius and Lysander around in circles in the woods, Oberon intends to go back to his queen. He will beg her for charge of the Indian boy and then take the spell off her so that she no longer loves Bottom in his donkey head. Puck warns Oberon that night is soon over so they'd both better be quick.

PUCK:

Up and down, up and down,
I will lead them up and down.

(Lysander and Demetrius now go back and forth across the stage—first one crosses the stage looking for the other, then EXITS, then the other crosses the stage and EXITS, several times.)

LYSANDER:

Where art thou, proud Demetrius? Speak!

PUCK:

(In hiding, disguising his voice, pretending to be Demetrius.)
Here, villain, drawn and ready!

LYSANDER:

I will be with you straight.

PUCK:

(In hiding, disguising his voice.)
Follow me, then, to plainer ground.

DEMETRIUS:

Lysander, speak again! Where are you?

PUCK:

(In hiding, disguising his voice, pretending to be Lysander.)
Thou coward!
And wilt thou not come?
I'll whip thee with a rod.

(ENTER LYSANDER.)

LYSANDER:

He goes before me and still dares me on.
When I come where he calls, then he is gone.
I have fallen in dark uneven way,
And here will rest me till gentle day.

(Lysander lies down and sleeps.)

PUCK:

(In hiding, disguising his voice.)
Ho ho ho! Coward, why com'st thou not?

(ENTER DEMETRIUS, not seeing Lysander.)

DEMETRIUS:

Nay then, you mock me.
I am faint and will measure my length on this cold bed,
But wait 'til daylight!

(Demetrius lies down and sleeps.)

(ENTER HELENA.)

HELENA:

O weary night. O long and tedious night.
Sleep, that sometimes shuts up sorrow's eye,
Steal me awhile from mine own company.

(Helena lies down and sleeps.)

PUCK:

Yet but three? Come one more.
Two of both kinds makes up four.

(ENTER HERMIA.)

HERMIA:

Here will I rest me till the break of day.
Heavens shield Lysander if they mean a fray.

(Hermia lies down and sleeps.)

PUCK:

When thou wak'st
Thou tak'st
True delight
In the sight
Of thy former lady's eye.
Jack shall have Jill;
Naught shall go ill.
And all shall be well.

(Puck applies the nectar to Lysander's eyes and EXITS, skipping.)

ACT IV
Scene 1

*(The four young lovers are still asleep onstage. ENTER OBERON,
TITANIA, BOTTOM, and FAIRIES. Oberon must be unseen by Titania
and the fairies. The fairies are attending Bottom, scratching his head
and decorating it with a wreath of flowers.)*

TITANIA:

Come, sit thee down upon this flowery bed. Let me kiss thy fair large
ears, my gentle joy.

BOTTOM:

Where's Peaseblossom?

PEASEBLOSSOM:

Ready.

BOTTOM:

Scratch my head, Peaseblossom. Where's Monsieur Cobweb?

COBWEB:

Ready.

BOTTOM:

Monsieur Cobweb, kill me a red-hipped humble-bee on the top of a thistle and bring me the honey-bag. Where's Mustardseed?

MUSTARDSEED:

Ready. What's your will.

BOTTOM:

Nothing, good monsieur, but to help Cobweb to scratch. I must go to the barber's, for methinks I am marvelous hairy about the face.

TITANIA:

Will you hear some music, my sweet love? Or say what thou desirest to eat.

BOTTOM:

Truly I would like a nice bundle of hay. I could munch some good, dry oats and some sweet hay. But pray, I feel sleep coming on.

TITANIA:

Sleep, thou. O, how I love thee! How I dote on thee! Fairies, begone—

(EXIT FAIRIES. Titania and Bottom fall asleep.)

(ENTER PUCK.)

OBERON:

Welcome, good Puck. See'st thou this sweet sight?
I do begin to pity her.
She begged my patience and let me have the boy.
And now I will undo this transformation and
Release my Fairy Queen.

(Oberon applies the nectar to Titania's eyes.)

Be as thou was meant to be
See as thou was meant to see.
Wake, Titania, wake you, my sweet queen.

TITANIA:

(Waking up.) My Oberon, what visions have I seen!
Methought I was enamored of a donkey!
Oh! How I do loathe the sight of him now.

(Oberon motions to Puck to remove the donkey's head from Bottom and Puck does.)

OBERON:

Sound music. *(MUSIC.)*
Come, my queen, take hands with me.
And rock the ground whereon these sleepers be.

(Titania and Oberon dance a simple dance.)

PUCK:

Fairy King, attend and mark—
I do hear the morning lark.

TITANIA:

Come, my lord, and in our flight
Tell me how it came this night
That I sleeping here was found
With these mortals on the ground.

(EXIT TITANIA, OBERON, PUCK, and FAIRIES.)

NARRATOR:

Now that the fairy king and queen have made peace with each other and Bottom looks like himself again, Oberon is satisfied. He tells Titania that tomorrow at midnight they will join all four of the young lovers at the marriage of Duke Theseus and Hippolyta. Meanwhile, guess who now wanders into this forest bedroom? Duke Theseus himself, plus Hippolyta. They have come to the forest to perform some May Day rituals before their wedding.

(Horn sounds offstage.)

(ENTER DUKE THESEUS, HIPPOLYTA, and EGEUS, plus any ATTENDANTS they have.)

DUKE THESEUS:

Soft! What nymphs are these?

EGEUS:

My lord, this is my daughter here asleep,
And this Lysander; this Demetrius is,
This Helena. I wonder why they are here together.

DUKE THESEUS:

No doubt they rose up early to observe
The rite of May. But speak, Egeus. Is not this the day
That Hermia should give answer of her choice?

EGEUS:

It is, my lord.

(The horns sound again and the four young people wake and sit up.)

DUKE THESEUS:

 I pray you all, stand up.

*(Demetrius and Helena stand up, holding hands. Lysander and Hermia
do the same.)*

DUKE THESEUS:

I know you, Lysander and Demetrius, are rival enemies.
How come this gentle harmony between you?

LYSANDER:

I came with Hermia here. Our intent was to be gone from Athens
Where we might escape the peril of its law—

EGEUS:

Enough, enough! I beg the law, upon his head,
They would have stolen away.
Demetrius, they would have defeated you and me.

DEMETRIUS:

My good lord, I know not by what power it is,
But my love for Hermia has
Melted as the snow.
The object and the pleasure of mine eye
Is only Helena.

DUKE THESEUS:

Fair lovers, you are fortunately met.
Of all this we will hear more anon.
By and by, with us,
These couples shall be wed.
Away with us to Athens. We'll hold a feast—come, Hippolyta.

(EXIT DUKE THESEUS, HIPPOLYTA, EGEUS, and ATTENDANTS.)

DEMETRIUS:

Are you sure we are awake? Let's follow him
And on the way, let us recount our dreams.

(EXIT THE FOUR LOVERS, happily, hand in hand.)

(Bottom wakes up.)

BOTTOM:

When my cue comes, call me, and I will answer.
Hey-ho! Peter Quince! Flute the bellows-mender! Snout the tinker!
Starveling! Where are they? Stolen away and left me asleep? I have had a
dream past the wit of man to say what it was.

(EXIT BOTTOM.)

NARRATOR:

Bottom goes off to find his friends, and I can assure you that Flute the
bellows-mender, Snout the tinker, Starveling, and Peter Quince are over-
joyed to see their old friend looking like himself again. They quickly make
their way to Athens so as to be sure to be on time for the wedding festivities.
They are determined to put on their play for the Duke.

ACT V
Scene 1

(HORN SOUNDS.)

*(ENTER DUKE THESEUS, HIPPOLYTA, PHILOSTRATE, and any
ATTENDANTS.)*

HIPPOLYTA:

'Tis strange, my Duke Theseus, what these lovers speak of.

DUKE THESEUS:

More strange than true. I never believe
These antique fables, nor these fairy toys.
Lovers and madmen have such seething brains—
But here come the lovers now.

(ENTER LYSANDER, HERMIA, DEMETRIUS, and HELENA.)

Joy, gentle friends! Joy and fresh days of love
Accompany your hearts!

(Everyone embraces and looks happy.)

DUKE THESEUS:

Come now, what revels shall we have
Is there no play to wear away the evening 'til bedtime?
Philostrate!

PHILOSTRATE:

There is a play, my lord,
The tragical tale of Pyramus and Thisbe,
Yet it made my eyes water with merry tears.

DUKE THESEUS:

We will hear it.

PHILOSTRATE:

No, my noble lord,
It is not for you. I have heard it over,
And it is nothing, nothing in the world.

DUKE THESEUS:

I will hear that play.

PHILOSTRATE:

So please your Grace.

(ENTER QUINCE first, bowing, followed by the OTHER PLAYERS, who bow in turn.)

QUINCE:

Gentles, perchance you wonder at this show.
But wonder on, till truth make all things plain.
This man is Pyramus, if you would know.

(Bottom as Pyramus bows pompously.)

This beauteous lady Thisbe is certain.

(Flute in a dress with a shawl, playing Thisbe, curtsys.)

And this man doth present "Wall."
Through Wall's chink, poor souls, these lovers did whisper.

(Play is done swiftly and silently as pantomime and the spectators clap and laugh throughout.)

(SNOUT, as WALL, walks in sideways, dressed in gray/brown.)

(STARVELING ENTERS as Moonshine—holding a lantern and leading a stuffed animal dog—and SNUG, as the Lion, ENTERS and roars loudly.)

(LION and MOONSHINE EXIT.)

(Pyramus struts around. Thisbe and Pyramus talk to each other "through" the Wall. THEY EXIT.)

(WALL EXITS.)

(MOONSHINE and LION RE-ENTER.)

(THISBE ENTERS. Lion roars and frightens her. THISBE EXITS, running off in fear, dropping her shawl. Lion picks up her shawl and shakes it in his mouth. Drops it.)

(LION EXITS.)

(PYRAMUS ENTERS. He finds Thisbe's shawl and thinks she is dead. Stabs himself.)

PYRAMUS/BOTTOM:
Now since lion vile hath killed my dear—she the fairest dame that lived—thus die I thus . . . thus . . . thus . . . *(Pretends to die.)* Now am I dead. Moon, take thy flight.

(Pyramus falls.)

(THISBE ENTERS and sees Pyramus. Stabs herself and falls.)

(Other PLAYERS RE-ENTER. Pyramus and Thisbe join them, all the PLAYERS BOW and EXIT.)

(The spectators clap and laugh.)

NARRATOR:

The Duke and Hippolyta and the four young people greatly enjoyed the play, but now it is almost midnight and everyone must say good night. Soon the fairies will be out.

DUKE THESEUS:

Sweet friends to bed.
For a fortnight hold we this festivity
In nightly revels and new jollity.

(EXIT the couples, two by two.)

(ENTER PUCK, followed by OBERON and TITANIA and ASSORTED FAIRIES, running around the stage as if they are flying, blessing the house.)

TITANIA:

Hand in hand, with fairy grace,
Will we sing and bless this place.

OBERON:

Now until the break of day,
Through this house each fairy stray.
The owner of it blest,
Ever shall in safety rest.

(Simple dance led by Oberon and Titania. MUSIC.)

OBERON:

Trip away. Make no stay.
Meet me all by break of day.

(EXIT ALL but Puck.)

PUCK:

If we shadows have offended,
Think but this and all is mended:
That you have but slumbered here
While these visions did appear.

(Puck dances or flits from one side of the stage to the other.)

NARRATOR:

Puck says we should think of the events we have just seen as a dream. He knows the story was hard to believe and he begs us to forgive the fairies.

PUCK:

So good night unto you all.
(Pantomimes clapping hands.)
Give me your hands, if we be friends,
And Puck shall restore amends.

(MUSIC.)

(PUCK EXITS.)

*A Midsummer
Night's Dream*

Macbeth

King Macbeth consults the witches. *This stage setting
shows a castle backdrop, candles on the banquet table,
and the simply dressed characters in the foreground.*

The play *Macbeth* ends with a murdered King Macbeth, his queen dead of madness and guilt, and a stage full of slaughtered Scottish soldiers. Why would anyone want to introduce this play to children?

This is a reasonable question, but the only real answer is that they love it. The murder and mayhem caused by power-hungry and ambitious people may hit close to home for adults; but for children the bloody, dark events are pure make-believe. A battlefield, a remote castle, mysterious witches on a dark, windy night, a midnight murder, a queen going mad—all these provide excitement and hold children's attention, whether they are watching or performing.

Macbeth starts with the aftermath of a battle in which the title character is celebrated and praised for his great valor in fighting off Celtic invaders. But Macbeth's unraveling begins immediately afterwards. He and Banquo, a fellow lord and friend, meet three witches, whose strange appearance and even stranger predictions frighten him.

Macbeth is uneasily attracted to the witches' prophecy that he will be king, though he cannot conceive of how that will come about. All too soon, he finds himself a murderer and his wife the ready accomplice to Duncan's murder. In a hurling downward spiral, Macbeth quickly changes from a triumphant hero to a tortured despot—a man who inflicts cruelty on others and who cannot save himself.

The 1100s in Scotland and England were a dark, suspicious time. People with all levels of education believed devoutly in witches and ghosts and were convinced that the supernatural was a powerful force. Children seem to grasp this notion right away, and they know there is a difference between that time and their own. They also understand that while many men and women act heroically and bravely, they can also reach too far.

The events of *Macbeth* are based on medieval Scottish history, although Shakespeare's work does not stick firmly to the facts. The historical Macbeth may have had reasons to want to kill King Duncan, for the real King Duncan was a usurper to the throne. In Shakespeare's play, though, Duncan is portrayed as a decent, blameless ruler.

Shakespeare's chief printed source for British and Roman history was a book called *Chronicles* by Raphael Holinshed, but Shakespeare was just as influenced by common lore and by other people's plays and stories. He wrote the play late in his career, probably around 1606 when James I, a Scottish king, had succeeded the long-reigning Queen Elizabeth on the English throne.

We blame Macbeth's downfall on his ambition, his fear, his confusion at the witches' prophecies, and his desire to satisfy his wife's entreaties that he act like a man. Whether Macbeth has a hand in his own fate or is merely its pawn is a question mature audiences may argue over. Children watching the play, however, generally do not concern themselves with why the events happen, simply that they do.

Suggested Music

Scotland's Music (compact disk). Linn Records, Linn Products Ltd., Glasgow. (*Note:* This CD is out of print but is available for legal download at www. linnrecords.com.)

Come, Gentle Night: Music of Shakespeare's World (compact disc). Ensemble Galilei, Telarc Records, 2000.

Other suggestions for music: bells, recorders and/or flutes, drums, trumpet fanfares.

Suggested Props

Hobby horses

Feast preparations: basket of fruit, other food

Goblets, pitcher, plates, tablecloth

Broad swords, dagger

Bell

Witches' cauldron and large spoon

Candle and candle holder

Tree branches

Suggested Backdrops

Castle

Forest

Suggested Costumes

Look for kilts or plaid skirts for the boys, or even just lengths of plaid or solid fabric wrapped around the lower half of the body and twisted up and tossed over the shoulder. Any sort of tunic will also work. (If they're playing medieval warriors, most boys will not balk at wearing something that looks like a skirt.) Leggings, high socks, or even bare legs are fine under the kilts. Warriors in medieval Scotland were not particularly clean, so neither costumes nor children need be pristine. King Duncan can have a crown and a cape. Lady Macbeth can wear a gown of some kind and, if possible, a white nightgown for the mad scene.

You can be very inventive and eclectic when it comes to dressing your witches, and they can be played by girls or boys. In the original, they are described by Banquo as appearing to be women but having beards. Leotards, scarves, raggedy dresses, leggings, T-shirts, and black robes—any and all of these will look great.

Cast of Characters

Narrator(s)

Witches (three to six)

King Duncan

Malcolm, son of Duncan

Captain

Donalbain, son of Duncan

Lennox, Scottish nobleman

Ross, Scottish nobleman

Angus, Scottish nobleman

Macbeth

Banquo

Lady Macbeth

Fleance, Banquo's son

Macduff

Murderers (two)

Soldiers

Hecate

Doctor

Attendant to Lady Macbeth

Messenger and/or servant

Pronunciation Guide to Names

Banquo (bang-kwoh)

Cawdor (caw-dawr)

Donalbain (dahn-uhl-bane)

Duncan (dung-ken)

Fleance (flay-ahns)

Hecate (heck-uh-tee)

Macbeth (mak-beth)

Malcolm (mal-kum)

Scenes

The heath, the castle, and the forest.

Macbeth

ACT I
Scene 1

Outdoors, semidark, foggy, and eerie.

(MUSIC.)

(ENTER NARRATOR AND WITCHES. There can be three or more witches, as needed for casting. Make adjustments to script and stage direction as necessary.)

FIRST WITCH:
When shall we three meet again?
In thunder, lightning, or in rain?

SECOND WITCH:
When the hurly-burly's done,
When the battle's lost and won.

THIRD WITCH:
That will be before the set of sun.

FIRST WITCH:
Where the place?

SECOND WITCH:
Upon the heath.

THIRD WITCH:
There to meet with Macbeth.

ALL WITCHES TOGETHER:
Fair is foul and foul is fair.
Hover through the fog and filthy air.

(EXIT WITCHES.)

(MUSIC.)

ACT I
Scene 2

Duncan's castle.

(ENTER DUNCAN, CAPTAIN, MALCOLM, DONALBAIN, and LENNOX. The Captain is bleeding, weak.)

NARRATOR:
Welcome, my friends, to medieval Scotland, to the Court of King Duncan. War has been raging across the heath as the Scottish thanes fight to turn back invaders from Ireland and Norway. Here in Duncan's court, word has just arrived that the battle is won. Messengers say that the mighty Macbeth fought valiantly to defend the Scottish king. No foe can stand against him.

KING DUNCAN:
What bloody man is that?
(Points at Captain.)

MALCOLM:
This is the sergeant
Who like a good and hardy soldier fought
Against my captivity. Hail, brave friend!

CAPTAIN:
All's too weak for brave Macbeth—well, he deserves that name.
He faced the villain my captor
never shook hands nor bade farewell to him
Till he unseamed him from the nave to the chaps
And fixed his head upon our battlements.

KING DUNCAN:
O valiant cousin, worthy gentleman!
So well thy words become thee as thy wounds,
They smack of honor both. Go get him surgeons.

(EXIT ALL.)

ACT I
Scene 3

On the heath.

(ENTER MACBETH and BANQUO on "horseback.")

NARRATOR:

Macbeth and Banquo are making their way home, where they know they will be welcome in the king's castle. But strange sounds and sights, and an eerie fog is dampening their great victory. The witches are about to stop Macbeth and Banquo and make some very strange predictions. Hark!

MACBETH:

So foul and fair a day I have not seen.

(MUSIC.)

(ENTER WITCHES.)

BANQUO:

Fouler still as the day goes on, Macbeth.
What are these so withered and so wild in their attire
That look not like inhabitants of the earth and yet are on it?

FIRST WITCH:

All hail Macbeth, Thane of Glamis! *(Croaking.)*

SECOND WITCH:

All hail Macbeth, Thane of Cawdor! *(Cackling.)*

THIRD WITCH:

All hail Macbeth, who shall one day be king! *(Hissing.)*

(Macbeth looks startled and frightened.)

BANQUO:

Why fear what sounds so fair? *(Turns to the three witches.)*
If you can look into the seeds of time
And say which grain will grow and which will not,
Then speak to me of what MY life shall be!

ALL WITCHES TOGETHER:

Hail!

FIRST WITCH:

Lesser than Macbeth, and greater.

SECOND WITCH:

Not so happy, yet much happier.

THIRD WITCH:

Thou shalt be the father of kings, though thou be none.

ALL WITCHES:

So all hail Macbeth and Banquo!

(MUSIC.)

(EXIT WITCHES.)

MACBETH:

Your children shall be kings!

BANQUO:

YOU shall be king!

MACBETH:

And thane of Cawdor too, went it not so?

(They travel on.)

(ENTER ROSS and ANGUS.)

ROSS:

Hail, Thane of Cawdor!

MACBETH:

Why do you dress me in borrowed robes? The Thane of Cawdor lives!

ANGUS:

Not for long. He has betrayed the king and is condemned to die.
His land and title come from Duncan's hand to thee,
In gratitude for your great deeds in battle.

BANQUO:

Be not too eager. Remember, the powers of darkness
May use a bit of truth to lure a man to doom.

MACBETH:

(Getting excited.) Come what may.
Time and the hour runs through the roughest day.
Let us toward the king!

(ALL EXIT.)

ACT I
Scene 4

Macbeth's castle.

NARRATOR:

In Dunsinane, the castle of King Duncan, Macbeth was met with much congratulation and praise. Macbeth has told the king that he wishes to go ahead to see his wife, Lady Macbeth, and ask her to prepare their own castle for a visit from the king. You might think that Macbeth's wife would be eager to extend her hospitality to the king and she is—but not in the way you would expect. Lady Macbeth has received a letter from her husband telling her about the strange prophecy that he would become king. Suddenly she wants her husband to be king so much that she is having murderous thoughts.

(ENTER LADY MACBETH, reading a letter.)

LADY MACBETH:

Yet I do fear your nature, my husband.
It is too full of the milk of human kindness
To catch the nearest way. I shall have to urge thee on.

(ENTER MACBETH. Lady Macbeth is startled but glad to see him.)

MACBETH:

My dearest love. Duncan comes here tonight.

LADY MACBETH:

Tonight! And when does he leave?

MACBETH:

Tomorrow.

LADY MACBETH

(Shaking her head.) Never shall tomorrow come, my lord.
Your face is like a book where I may read strange matters.
Let no one else see. Look like the innocent flower,
But be the serpent under it. Leave all the rest to me.

(EXIT MACBETH and LADY MACBETH. Various people in their castle carry in preparations for feast. Music plays. Bustling about.)

(ENTER LADY MACBETH. KING ENTERS. Lady Macbeth greets the King.)

KING DUNCAN:

Fair and noble hostess, we are your guest tonight.
Give me your hand. Conduct me to mine host; we love him highly
And shall continue our graces toward him.
By your leave, hostess.

(ALL EXIT except Narrator.)

NARRATOR:

The idea of murdering his king so that he can become the king himself is obsessing Macbeth. He is afraid to do it, knowing that the king is a good king and is also his guest and kinsman. Macbeth tells his wife that they should bar the door against Duncan's murderer—NOT bear the knife themselves! But she tells him not to be a coward. She says that tonight after Duncan is asleep, she will bring a potion to his guards that will make them fall asleep. And after she and Macbeth have killed Duncan, the guards will be blamed for Duncan's murder.

(ENTER MACBETH.)

MACBETH:

If it were done, would be well
To do it quickly . . .

(He paces back and forth.)

The king is here in double trust:
First, I am his kinsman and his subject,
Then, I am his host.
I should shut the door against his murderer,
Not bear the knife myself—

(ENTER LADY MACBETH.)

MACBETH:

We will proceed no further in this business!

LADY MACBETH:

Would you live a coward in your own esteem,
Letting "I dare not" wait upon "I would"?

MACBETH:

I pray thee, peace.
I dare do all that may become a man—no more.

LADY MACBETH:

What made you bring this idea to me?
When you did, THEN you were a man.

MACBETH:

And if we should fail?

LADY MACBETH:

Fail?
Are you afraid to claim your greatness?
Screw your courage to the sticking place!

MACBETH:

I am settled upon this terrible deed.
Away, and mock the time with fairest show.
False face must hide what the false heart doth know.

ACT II
Scene 1

(ENTER BANQUO and FLEANCE.)

NARRATOR:

The celebration and feasting are over. Macbeth's friend Banquo is unsettled and suspicious. He can't put his finger on what is bothering him and why he feels so agitated.

BANQUO:

How goes the night, boy?

FLEANCE:

The moon is down; I have not heard the clock.

BANQUO:

And she goes down at twelve.

FLEANCE:

I take it, it's later, sir.

(ENTER MACBETH and SERVANT, with a torch.)

BANQUO:

Who's there?

MACBETH:

A friend.

BANQUO:

What, sir, not yet at rest? The king's abed. I dreamt last night of the three weird sisters. To you they have showed some truth.

NARRATOR:

Macbeth is feeling suspicious of Banquo. He and Banquo bid each other an uneasy good night. Macbeth gets ready to deliver a very famous speech.

(EXIT BANQUO, SERVANT, and FLEANCE.).

MACBETH:

Is this a dagger I see before me, the handle toward my hand?
Come, let me clutch thee.
I have thee not, and yet I see thee still.

(Sound of a bell.)

MACBETH:

I go and it is done. The bell invites me.
Hear it not, Duncan, for it is a knell
That summons thee to heaven, or to hell.

(EXIT MACBETH.)

ACT II
Scene 2

(MUSIC.)

(A pantomime of the drugging of the guards and the killing of Duncan now takes place. The body of Duncan stays onstage. A cry is heard from offstage saying, "Sleep no more. Macbeth doth murder sleep!" An owl shrieks.)

NARRATOR:

Macbeth is very upset after he does this terrible act. He leaves the scene of the crime and goes to his wife. Not knowing what he is doing, he brings the bloody daggers with him.

(ENTER MACBETH and LADY MACBETH. Macbeth carries the bloody daggers.)

LADY MACBETH:

Why did you bring these with you? Get some water and wash this filthy witness from your hands.

MACBETH:

I'll go no more. I am afraid to think what I have done.

LADY MACBETH:

Infirm of purpose! Give me the daggers!

(Loud knocking sound from offstage.)

MACBETH:

Whence is that knocking?
Why is it that every noise appalls me?
What hands are these? Ha!
This hand will turn the green seas red.

LADY MACBETH:

My hands are of your color, but I shame
To wear a heart so white.

(Knocking again.)

LADY MACBETH:

I hear a knocking at the south entry.
Let us go to our chamber.
A little water clears us of this deed.
How easy it is then!

MACBETH:

To know my deed, it would be best not to know myself.

(Knocking again.)

I would we could wake Duncan with thy knocking!

(EXIT MACBETH and LADY MACBETH.)

ACT II
Scene 3

(Loud knocking coming from outside the castle. ENTER MACDUFF and LENNOX. ENTER MACBETH to greet them.)

MACDUFF:

Good morrow, sir. The king did command me to call timely on him.
I have almost slipped the hour.

MACBETH:

I will bring you to him.

This is the door. *(Points offstage in direction of King Duncan.)*

(MACDUFF EXITS.)

LENNOX:

The night has been unruly.

Chimneys were blown down

And strange screams of death seemed to fill the air.

MACBETH:

Twas a rough night.

(MACDUFF RE-ENTERS.)

MACDUFF:

Oh horror, horror, horror! Confusion now hath made his masterpiece!

Ring the alarm bell! Rouse the house! Murder and treason!

(General confusion. ENTER the king's sons MALCOLM and DONALBAIN, LADY MACBETH, BANQUO, and LENNOX.)

DONALBAIN:

What is amiss?

MACDUFF:

Your royal father's murdered.

MALCOLM:

By whom?

MACDUFF:

It would seem the very men who were pledged to guard him.

LENNOX:

Those of his chamber, it seems have done it.

Their hands and faces were all badged with blood.

MACBETH:

Oh, I do repent me of my fury

That I did kill them.

Who could be loyal to the king and neutral, in a moment?

LADY MACBETH:

Oh, help me hence! *(She swoons, as if about to faint.)*

MACDUFF:

Look to the lady.

(EXIT ALL but Malcolm and Donalbain.)

(Malcolm and Donalbain move aside, talking to each other quietly as Narrator speaks.)

NARRATOR:

Macduff, Lennox, and the king's sons are all very upset over the deed. Macbeth confesses that he killed the guards because he was so upset over the king's murder and thought they committed it. Macduff is suspicious of him, but says nothing. Meanwhile the king's sons decide that they will be suspected of the murder and they are also afraid for their own lives, so they decide to go away.

MALCOLM:

Our father's murderer may want our blood as well.

DONALBAIN:

In this place there are daggers in men's smiles. I'll go to Ireland.

MALCOLM:

And I to England.

(EXIT MALCOLM and DONALBAIN, running.)

ACT III
Scene 1

NARRATOR:

There is unruliness and unrest in the Scottish court. The Scottish thanes, or rulers, are suspicious of the king's sons, Malcolm and Donalbain, because they have run away. They choose their greatest warrior—Macbeth—to be their king.

(Pantomime of Macbeth being crowned.)

Macduff left before the coronation because he is suspicious of the new King Macbeth. Macbeth does not rest easy in his new castle. He knows that one man has reason to suspect him of murder: his old friend, Banquo, who had witnessed the weird sisters' prophecy that he would be king. And Macbeth cannot forget their words foretelling that Banquo—not he—would be the father of kings.

(ENTER KING MACBETH, BANQUO, SERVANT, and TWO MURDERERS.)

KING MACBETH:

(Aside to the audience.) For Banquo's children have I sold my soul!
For them have I murdered the gracious Duncan!
(To Banquo.) Tonight we hold a solemn supper, sir.
And I'll request your presence.

BANQUO:

Let your highness command upon me.

MACBETH:

Fail not our feast.

BANQUO:

My lord, I will not.

(EXIT BANQUO.)

MACBETH:

Our fears in Banquo stick deep.
And in his royalty of nature reigns that
Which would be feared.
(To the murderers.)
Both of you know Banquo was your enemy.

MURDERER 1:

True, my lord.

MURDERER 2:

We shall, my lord, perform what you command us.

MACBETH:

I'll call upon you straight. Abide within.
(Loudly, as if warning Banquo, though Banquo is not there.)
It is concluded, Banquo, thy soul's flight,
If it find heaven, must find it out tonight!

(ALL EXIT except Narrator.)

NARRATOR:

King Macbeth's power has gone to his head, but it's not making him happy. He is going crazy with suspicion and fear—why else would he be willing to kill his closest friend? Macbeth has the murderers follow Banquo and his son when they go riding through the countryside in the afternoon before the evening's banquet. The murderers do their grisly deed on Banquo, but there's one problem: Banquo's son, Fleance, escapes.

(From offstage hear cries and thumps—signs that murder is taking place.)

ACT III
Scene 2

(ENTER LADY MACBETH, KING MACBETH, LENNOX, ROSS, and OTHER LORDS, if available, for banquet. They sit at a table and hoist their goblets, etc.)

NARRATOR:

Macbeth was glad to hear that Banquo is dead, but he was not pleased when he heard that Fleance escaped the murderers. Now he has to live in fear of him too! At the banquet he cannot have a good time, and when a surprise guest shows up, Macbeth is the only one who can see him. It is the Ghost of Banquo!

(ENTER GHOST OF BANQUO, who drifts around and then sits down on an empty chair. The others look right through the Ghost of Banquo and don't know what's the matter with King Macbeth.)

(Macbeth starts and cries out.)

MACBETH:

Which of you has done this?

LENNOX:

What, my good lord?

MACBETH:

Thou can not say I did it. Never shake your gory locks at me!

ROSS:

Gentleman, rise. His highness is not well.

(BANQUO'S GHOST EXITS and Macbeth tries to sit down, but the party is breaking up.)

(EXIT ALL.)

NARRATOR:

Over the next few months, Macbeth learns that getting to be king by killing others is not a recipe for happiness. And it does not bring peace to the land. In his kingdom, rebellion is growing. He has no idea where Banquo's son Fleance is. Macbeth hears a rumor that King Duncan's son Malcolm is trying to stir up trouble against him in England. Macbeth thinks it's time to consult again with the witches.

ACT III

Scene 3

The heath.

(MUSIC.)

(The scene is the windy, eerie, foggy heath again. ENTER WITCHES, this time with HECATE.)

NARRATOR:

Not only has there been trouble in the kingdom, but there have also been problems brewing in the witches' world. The witches who made their strange predictions to Macbeth in the beginning of the play never got permission from their mistress, Hecate, and now they're in a spot of trouble.

FIRST WITCH:

How now, Hecate? You look angerly.

HECATE:

Have I not reason, beldams as you are?
Saucy and overbold? How did you dare
To trade and traffic with Macbeth
In riddles and affairs of death?
And I was never called to bear MY part?
Or show the glory of our art?

(She scolds them, and the witches get their cauldron out and start stirring.)

FIRST WITCH:

Thrice the brindled cat hath mewed.

SECOND WITCH:

Thrice, and once the hedgepig whined.

THIRD WITCH:

Harpier cries—'Tis time, 'tis time!

ALL WITCHES:

Double, double, toil and trouble
Fire burn and cauldron bubble.
Eye of newt and toe of frog
Wool of bat and tongue of dog
For a charm of powerful trouble
Like a hell-broth boil and bubble.

(EXIT ALL.)

ACT IV
Scene 1

(MUSIC.)

(ENTER HECATE with WITCHES.)

HECATE:

Oh, well done! I commend your pains
And every one shall share in the gains.
And now about the cauldron sing
Like elves and fairies in a ring
Enchanting all that you put in.

(MUSIC and a SIMPLE CIRCLE DANCE.)

Black spirits and white
Red spirits and gray
Mingle, mingle, mingle
You that mingle may.

Around, around, around, about, about
All ill come running in, all good keep out.

(ENTER MACBETH.)

MACBETH:

How now, you secret midnight hags!
What is it you do?

WITCHES:

A deed without a name!

NARRATOR:

Macbeth has come with questions. He demands that the witches answer him even if the answers will cause chaos and confusion. The witch sisters promise they'll answer, but they say Macbeth can either hear the answers from them or from their masters. Macbeth says he wants to see the masters, and suddenly an armored head appears. He tells Macbeth, in a ghostly voice, to "Beware the Thane of Fife!" The Thane of Fife is Macduff. Next, a child with a crown appears, holding a small tree.

(These apparitions can speak from backstage or they can appear onstage and speak.)

(MUSIC fading in and out.)

(Armored head appears.)

ARMORED HEAD:

Macbeth, Macbeth, Macbeth! Beware the Thane of Fife!

(Second apparition appears—child wearing crown and holding small tree.)

CHILD:

Macbeth shall never vanquished be, 'til Great Birnam Wood to high Dunsinane Hill shall come against him!

(Across back of stage slowly walk Duncan and Banquo, as if they are ghosts in the shadows.)

(ENTER MESSENGER.)

MESSENGER:

My lord! Macduff has fled to England!

MACBETH:

I should have acted the moment I suspected him!
Go to Fife. Enter Macduff's castle. Put the traitor's wife and babes
to the sword!

(EXIT ALL.)

ACT IV
Scene 2

England.

NARRATOR:

In his confusion, rage, and fear, Macbeth keeps making terrible mistakes. If he ever was a good man, he has completely lost his character by now. Hearing that he is supposed to fear the Thane of Fife, he reacts crazily. He orders that Macduff's wife and children be put to death. When the news of Macduff's family tragedy reaches him, Macduff is in England trying to convince King Duncan's son Malcolm to come home to Scotland and reclaim his father's throne.

(ENTER MACDUFF and MALCOLM. Macduff is obviously grief-stricken.)

MACDUFF:

My children too? My wife?
All my pretty ones? Did you say all? *(He weeps.)*
Oh, now bring me front to front with this fiend of Scotland!

MALCOLM:

Come, go we to the king. Our power is ready.
Receive what cheer you may. Let us make medicines of our great revenge to cure this deadly grief.

(EXIT ALL.)

ACT V
Scene 1

Macbeth's castle.

(ENTER LADY MACBETH, walking in her sleep and muttering to herself. She holds a candle. ENTER HER SERVANT and DOCTOR, talking to each other quietly and watching her. Lady Macbeth sets down the candle and rubs her hands together vigorously as if she is washing them.)

NARRATOR:

Apparently, murder was not as simple as Lady Macbeth thought it would be. The guilt has caught up to her, and she is not well. Her servant has called in a doctor to observe her.

LADY MACBETH:

Out, damned spot! Out, I say! Who would have thought the old man to have had so much blood in him? What, will these hands never be clean? Here's the smell of blood still. Oh, all the perfumes of Arabia will not sweeten this little hand!

DOCTOR:

This disease is beyond my practice.

LADY MACBETH:

To bed, to bed. There's knocking at the gate. Come, come, come, come, give me your hand. What's done cannot be undone. To bed, to bed, to bed.

DOCTOR:

Will she go now to bed?

ATTENDANT:

Directly.

DOCTOR:

(To the attendant.) Foul whisperings are about.
Unnatural deeds breed unnatural troubles.
I fear your lady's hands will not be made clean by any medicine.
God, God forgive us all . . . Look after her.

ATTENDANT:

Good night, good doctor.

(EXIT ALL.)

ACT V
Scene 2

Army forces are gathering outside the castle.

NARRATOR:

The English king sent an army with Malcolm and Macduff to help overturn the tyrant King Macbeth. The soldiers are now gathering in the forest outside Macbeth's castle. Macbeth's spies had told him the soldiers were coming, but he wasn't worried. After all, he understood the witches' prophecy to say that he would never be vanquished until Birnam Wood came to Dunsinane. He knew—or thought he knew—that a forest could not move on its own.

MACBETH:

Bring me no more reports. Till Birnam Wood remove to Dunsinane—
I cannot fear that. The boy Malcolm I cannot fear;
He'll never have power of me.
The mind I sway by and the heart I bear
Shall never sag with doubt nor shake with fear.

(ENTER MACBETH and MESSENGER.)

MACBETH:

Speak, thou cream-faced loon!
Where from, that goose look?

MESSENGER:

There is ten thousand—

MACBETH:

Geese, villain?

MESSENGER:

Soldiers, sir!

MACBETH:

Go, thou lily-livered boy! What soldiers, patch?
Death of thy soul! What soldiers, whey-face?

MESSENGER:

English soldiers!

MACBETH:

Get thy face away!

(EXIT MESSENGER.)

MACBETH:

I have lived long enough. I'll fight till from my bones my flesh be hacked.
Where is my armor? *(He looks about for his armor. Puts it on.)*

(Cries of women from backstage. Macbeth is startled.)

NARRATOR:

Macbeth is worried about Lady Macbeth, who he thinks is dying of guilt.
He straps on his armor and goes off to battle her sorrow.

(EXIT MACBETH.)

(ENTER MALCOLM and SOLDIERS with branches held in front of their faces.)

MALCOLM:

Hold the branch before you. Thus we will approach Dunsinane without Macbeth knowing our true numbers!

(They march across the stage and off the stage.)

(ENTER MACBETH and SOLDIERS. ENTER MESSENGER.)

MESSENGER:

The queen, my lord, is dead!

(EXIT MESSENGER.)

MACBETH:

Tomorrow, and tomorrow, and tomorrow
Creeps in this petty pace from day to day
To the last syllable of recorded time,
And all our yesterdays have lighted fools
The way to dusty death. Out, out, brief candle
Life's but a walking shadow, a poor player
That struts and frets his hour upon the stage
And then is heard no more. It is a tale
Told by an idiot, full of sound and fury,
Signifying nothing.

(MESSENGER ENTERS, running.)

MESSENGER:

The woods have begun to move!

MACBETH:

Liar and slave!

(ENTER MACDUFF.)

MACDUFF:

Turn, you hound! Turn!

MACBETH:

Lay on, Macduff!

(Grunts and groans. Macduff kills Macbeth.)

(ENTER MALCOLM, NOBLEMEN, and SOLDIERS.)

MACDUFF:

Hail, King, for so thou art!

ALL:

Hail, King of Scotland!

MALCOLM:

Let us call home our exiled friends abroad
That fled the snares of tyranny.
So ends our tale of this dead butcher
And his fiendlike queen.
By the grace of Grace
We will perform in measure, time, and place.
So thanks to all at once and to each one,
Whom we invite to see us crowned at Scone.

(MUSIC.)

(EXIT ALL.)

Macbeth

King Henry IV, Part I

Falstaff and the tavern hostess enjoy a joke at the inn.

Falstaff is an easy character to dress: Use a little padding under
the child's shirt and create boots by wrapping fabric around
the lower leg and over the tops of the shoes.
Mistress Quickly, the hostess, just needs an apron.

T his is a wonderful play. In the opinion of many, it is Shakespeare's best history play, with lively characters and plenty of comedy in its famous tavern scenes. These scenes balance more serious scenes at court and on the battlefield. Although it deals with weighty political and historical matters, *King Henry IV, Part I* is not hard to follow, and it can be appreciated by young people on one level and by older audiences in a deeper way.

Based loosely on events during the reign of King Henry IV—almost two hundred years before his time—Shakespeare wrote the play around 1596, as part of a four-play series.

The play is about honor at home and on the battlefield, and it is also about growing up. When it opens, King Henry IV is intent on mounting a crusade to the Holy Land, but it soon becomes clear that this is wishful thinking: Events much closer to home command his attention. There are uprisings in both Wales and Scotland, and these rebellions may force the king into war. Edmund Mortimer has been taken prisoner by the Welsh and a thousand of his men killed. In Scotland, Henry Percy, nicknamed Hotspur, is heralded as a great hero for having taken many Scottish prisoners.

Hearing this news, King Henry reluctantly makes a comparison between the valiant and impetuous Hotspur and his own son, Prince Hal. About the same age as Hotspur, Hal has scarcely been the model of an upstanding prince. Instead, the prince spends his time and money in taverns, carousing with his friend Sir John Falstaff, a man old enough to know better. Jack Falstaff is fat, often drunk, cowardly, and clever—and he is one of Shakespeare's most memorable characters. Falstaff loves life. He doesn't shrink from crime, either, and readily engages in thievery. In Hal Falstaff has found a young protégé who shares his laziness and his drinking, but also his quick wit and fondness for schemes.

Back at court it becomes all too clear that Hotspur and the rest of the Percy family are plotting a rebellion against their king. They resent him for not showing them enough gratitude when they helped him seize the throne and kill the former king. Observing the gathering strength of this resentment against his father, Prince Hal decides now is the time for action. He pits himself against the hot-headed and hot-blooded Hotspur and helps to quash the rebellion, at least temporarily.

Saving his father's life and his family's honor is the method by which Hal renounces childish things. Children can understand that Hal's personal reform is a process and also a choice. At first they laugh at the tavern scenes and thrill to the battle scenes. But they'll learn quickly that this play is not black and white, not right versus wrong. When Falstaff devises a plan to rob pilgrims on their way to Canterbury, in Act II, kids sense that he is going too far. When Hal thwarts their plan and in turn robs Falstaff, they laugh because it's funny, but also with relief that Hal is not as bad as his friend. When the time comes for Hal to grow up, they will see that he does not turn his back on his old friends in the process.

By the end of this play, it is too soon to tell what the young prince will be like as a ruler or even what will happen to the current rebellions. In terms of history, the play doesn't "solve" anything. It does, however, show Hal's desire to think for himself. He decides not to accept Hotspur's notion of honor or Falstaff"s—both wrongheaded in their own ways—but to develop his own.

Suggested Music

Come, Gentle Night: Music of Shakespeare's World (compact disc). Ensemble Galilei, Telarc Records, 2000.

Other suggestions for music: any medieval or Celtic music, featuring the harp, guitar, flute, and recorder.

Suggested Props

Swords

Armor (simple breast plates and shields out of plastic or cardboard)

Mugs, bottles, plates for tavern scenes

Hobby horses

Rope

Blindfolds
Sheets of paper for bills, receipts
Purses or small sacks

Suggested Backdrops

Castle

Outdoor scene for battlefield and traveling/robbery scenes

Plain walls for tavern

Suggested Costumes

The young men can wear leggings or pants and belted tunics (blouses or shirts). Jack Falstaff should be padded to look portly. High boots and a brimmed tall hat would complete his look. The king should somehow be distinguished from the other men by a cape, crown, or royal garb. Ladies can wear simple gowns or dresses.

Cast of Characters

Narrator(s)

The court
    King Henry IV
    Prince Hal, son of Henry and heir to the throne (sometimes called Harry)
    Prince John, the King's younger son
    Earl of Westmoreland, a nobleman and friend to the King
    Sir Walter Blunt

The rebel camp
    Earl of Worcester, Hotspur's uncle (called Thomas Percy)
    Earl of Northumberland, Hotspur's father (called Henry Percy)
    Hotspur, Henry Percy the younger
    Earl of Douglas (called Douglas)
    Owen Glendower (called the wild Welshman)
    Lady Percy, Hotspur's wife and Mortimer's sister (called Kate)
    Lady Mortimer, Glendower's daughter
    Hotspur's servant
    Sir Richard Vernon, Hotspur's cousin
    Messengers/soldiers in Hotspur's army

The tavern
    Sir John Falstaff (sometimes called Jack)
    Poins
    Tavern mates, partners in crime (two)
    Travelers (two)
    Mistress Quickly, hostess of the tavern
    Tavern servant

Pronunciation Guide to Names

    Owen Glendower (oh-un glen-dow-er)
    Falstaff (fall-staff)
    Mortimer (mawr-tuh-mer)
    Northumberland (nawr-thuhm-ber-luhnd)
    Phoebus (fee-bus)
    Poins (poynz)
    Worcester (woos-ter)

Scenes

    Court, tavern, and battlefield.

King Henry IV, Part I

ACT I
Scene 1

The court.

(ENTER NARRATOR.)

NARRATOR:

Welcome to our production of *King Henry IV, Part I*. William Shakespeare wrote plays that were comic and plays that were tragic. He also wrote a lot about history. People in sixteenth-century England had a great hunger for history. It was very exciting and mysterious to them to hear about people and places long ago and far away. It was also very exciting for them to hear about the historical events in their own country. These were people who didn't have books, newspapers, and magazines, not to mention television and the Internet keeping them constantly informed. Going to the theater and seeing live on the stage the reenactment of their country's colorful history was great entertainment—and educational too!

In *King Henry IV, Part 1*, Shakespeare wrote about a time almost two centuries before his own time. This play was written during the fourth decade of Queen Elizabeth's long reign, in the late 1590s. But in the play Shakespeare was writing about events that took place about 170 years earlier than that—in 1420 or so.

In this first scene you will see King Henry IV. He hasn't been king that long. In fact, some say that he became king unfairly—by grabbing power from others. That wasn't so unusual in those days, or perhaps in any day. But at the start of our play, King Henry is ready to be a good king and serve his people, as he expects them to serve him in turn. He is thinking now that he would like to mount a crusade to Jerusalem, in the ongoing pursuit of dominating the world with Christianity. But this ambitious plan is about to be interrupted by events much closer to home. Fights are continuing on the borders with Wales and with Scotland.

(ENTER KING HENRY, PRINCE JOHN, and EARL OF WESTMORELAND.)

KING:

So shaken as we are, so wan with care,
Let us find time like a tired animal does—panting,
But ready for new battles in lands far off.

WESTMORELAND:

Yes, my liege.

KING:

No more shall we spill our children's blood on this soil
Plowing war into our own fields.
Let us now to the tomb of Christ
And bring the English power
To chase those pagans in the holy fields
Walked on by Christ's blessed feet
Fourteen hundred years ago.
Gentle cousin Westmoreland,
What did our council say yesterday
In forwarding this expedition?

WESTMORELAND:

There is heavy news from Wales.
The noble Mortimer who was leading a battle against the wild Welshman
Glendower is captured and a thousand of his people butchered.

KING:

It seems then that the tidings of this broil
Brake off our business for the Holy Land.

WESTMORELAND:

More uneven and unwelcome news came from the north, from
Rebellious Scotland, my gracious lord.
The gallant Hotspur and brave Archibald met at Holmedon
And spent a sad and bloody hour.

KING:

But we have also more smooth and welcome news.
The Earl of Douglas is defeated.
Walter saw ten thousand bold Scots piled up in their
Own blood, two-and-twenty knights dead.
The gallant Hotspur took many Scottish prisoners.
Is this not an honorable spoil, cousin?

WESTMORELAND:

In faith, it is a conquest for a prince to boast of.

KING:

It makes me sad and envious that Lord Northumberland
Should be blessed with such a son as Henry Percy,
The Brave Hotspur, while riot and dishonor
Stain the brow of our own Prince Hal.
But what think you of this young Percy's pride?
He says I shall have none of his prisoners
But Mordake, Earl of Fife.

WESTMORELAND:

This is his uncle's teaching. This is Worcester.
Worcester means evil to you in all respects.

KING:

I have sent for Hotspur to answer this.
Meanwhile we must put aside our holy purpose in Jerusalem.
We will hold council Wednesday at Windsor.

(EXIT KING and WESTMORELAND.)

NARRATOR:

The king is proud of the great young warrior Harry Percy, known as Hotspur, but he is jealous. He would really like his own son, Prince Hal, to be as brave and successful in battle as Hotspur. Prince Hal is a generous, intelligent young man who up until now has shown very little ambition. He likes to have a good time, and in this next scene you will meet him, along with his friend Sir John Falstaff—an older man who would be considered a bad influence by most parents. The two of them are frequently seen in taverns and like to hang around together, joking and carrying on. Worse than that, they have also been known to steal from people.

ACT I
Scene 2

A tavern.

(ENTER FALSTAFF and PRINCE HAL.)

FALSTAFF:

Now Hal, what time of day is it, lad?

PRINCE HAL:

Thou art so fat-headed with drinking and too much supper and sleeping upon benches after noon . . . why the devil do you need to know what time it is?

FALSTAFF:

Indeed, Hal, for we that take purses go by the moon and the seven stars . . . and not by Phoebus, god of the sun. Let us be gentlemen of the shade, minions of the moon, and let men say we be men of good government.

PRINCE:

Thou sayst well. Where shall we steal a purse tomorrow, Jack?

(ENTER POINS.)

FALSTAFF:

Poins! Here is a true villain!

PRINCE:

Good morrow, Ned.

POINS:

Good morrow, sweet Hal. What says Sir John Sack and Sugar? *(Poins nods to Falstaff.)* My lads, tomorrow morning at four o'clock at Gad's Hill there are pilgrims going to Canterbury with rich offerings, and traders riding to London with fat purses. We may have them as sure as sleep. I have ordered supper tomorrow in Eastcheap. We'll meet there. If you will go, I'll stuff your purses full of crowns; if you do not, stay at home and be hanged!

FALSTAFF:

Hal, wilt thou?

PRINCE:

Who, I rob? I a thief? Not I!

FALSTAFF:

Why, there is no honesty, manhood, nor good fellowship in thee, nor royal blood, if you dare not fight for ten shillings!

PRINCE:
(Shaking his head.)
Nay, come what will, I'll stay at home.

POINS:

Sir John, leave the prince and me alone. I will give him such reasons for this adventure that he shall go.

FALSTAFF:

Well, God give thee the spirit of persuasion and him the ears to profit by it. Farewell, you shall find me in Eastcheap.

(EXIT FALSTAFF.)

POINS:

Now, my good sweet honey lord, ride with us tomorrow. I have a trick to play that I can't manage alone.

(Poins and the Prince wander off to the side of stage, talking about the plan. Poins must look like he is trying to convince Hal.)

NARRATOR:

Poins has some pretty good mischief in mind. Prince Hal is doubtful, but he allows himself to be persuaded. Poins tells Hal that they will set up a time and place to meet Falstaff and the others, but then they won't show up. Falstaff will hold up the travelers and steal their money as planned, at which point—surprise!—Hal and Poins will attack them. Hal points out that of course Falstaff and his friends will recognize their horses and their clothes and every other detail of their appearance. Poins says no, they will leave their horses tied up in the woods, and they will change their appearance.

(Characters move forward.)

POINS:

The best part of this trick is the lies our fat friend will tell us when he meets us for supper—how he fought off thirty men at least.

PRINCE:

Well, I'll go with thee. Get everything ready and meet me tomorrow night in Eastcheap. Farewell.

POINS:

Farewell, my lord.

(EXIT POINS.)

NARRATOR:

In this next speech Prince Hal talks directly to the audience—or to himself. He says he'll go along with his friends for a while, but not for long. He compares himself to the sun being covered up by dark clouds: It may seem dark now, but pretty soon the clouds will part and the sun will shine. In other words, he may seem reckless and lazy now, but soon he will surprise everyone and show his true worth.

PRINCE:

> I know you all, and will awhile uphold
>
> The unyoked humor of your idleness.
>
> Yet in this way I will imitate the sun
>
> Who permits the dark clouds
>
> To smother up his beauty from the world.
>
> If all the year were playing holidays,
>
> To sport would be as tedious as to work
>
> But when they seldom come, they wished-for come.
>
> So, when I throw off this loose behavior
>
> My change will show more goodly and attract more eyes.
>
> I'll so offend to make offense a skill,
>
> Redeeming time when men think least I will.

(EXIT PRINCE HAL.)

ACT I
Scene 3

The court.

NARRATOR:

We now return to the king and his men. Against his will, the king finds himself in the middle of a rivalry between his family and the Percy family. The Percys helped him get to the throne by overthrowing the last king, and now they appear to be turning against him. In this next scene, you will see the Lord Northumberland—a Percy—and his son, the gallant warrior Hotspur.

(ENTER KING, NORTHUMBERLAND, and HOTSPUR.)

KING:

> My blood has been too cold and temperate,
>
> Unapt to stir at these indignities. I have lost respect.
>
> But you tread upon my patience and now I will
>
> Henceforth be myself
>
> Mighty and to be feared.

WORCESTER:

> The house of Percy, my lord, does not deserve this punishment
>
> From your greatness, which we have helped to build.

KING:

Worcester, get thee gone, for I do see

Danger and disobedience in your eye.

When we need you, we will send for you.

Now—Northumberland? You were about to speak.

NORTHUMBERLAND:

Yea, my good lord. My son Harry does not refuse your highness those prisoners he took in your name at Holmedon. Either envy or mistake has made it seem so, but not my son.

HOTSPUR:

(Defensive, provoked.) My liege, I did deny no prisoners!

But when the fight was done,

When I was dry with rage and extreme toil,

Breathless and leaning upon my sword,

Came there a certain lord neat and trimly dressed,

Fresh as a bridegroom, perfumed like a milliner,

Taking in snuff.

He smiled and talked and as the soldiers bore dead bodies by.

He called them unmannerly fools and demanded my prisoners.

(Hotspur mimics a fancy-dressed lord taking snuff from a snuff box and picking his way disdainfully through a field of dead bodies.)

Pestered with such a popinjay,

Out of my grief and impatience, I said I know not what.

(As Narrator speaks following lines, king and the others should move back and argue among themselves.)

NARRATOR:

Hotspur is angry that one of the King's men showed up on the battlefield and took it for granted that Hotspur would turn over the prisoners he had just taken. The King is angry because Hotspur has demanded a ransom for these prisoners: He insists that the king free his brother-in-law, Mortimer. Mortimer is married to a Welsh woman, daughter of the man everyone refers to as "the wild Glendower."

KING:

But he does deny me his prisoners

By making them ransom for the foolish Mortimer!

Should our coffers be emptied to bring home revolted Mortimer?

HOTSPUR:

Revolted Mortimer? But he never did betray you, my sovereign liege. He fought Glendower alone for the best part of an hour and has the wounds to show for it.

KING:

(Angrily.)
You lie, Percy, you lie!
He never did encounter with Glendower.
My lord Northumberland,
We ask that you depart with your son.
Send us your prisoners or you will hear of it.

(EXIT KING.)

HOTSPUR:

And if the devil roars for them
I will not send them!
I'll keep them all! He shall not have a Scot of them!

(ENTER WORCESTER.)

WORCESTER:

Hear you, cousin, a word.

HOTSPUR:

All I care for now is how to gall and pinch this king
And his son the Prince of Wales.
If I thought his father loved him
I would have poisoned him with a pot of ale.

NORTHUMBERLAND:

What a wasp-stung and impatient fool you are!
You tie your ear to no tongue but your own—

(EXIT HOTSPUR. WORCESTER and NORTHUMBERLAND EXIT, talking and trying to make Hotspur listen.)

NARRATOR:

Hotspur's uncle and his father plead with Hotspur to settle down and listen to what they have to say. Finally he agrees. They explain that the reason the king is so upset about Mortimer is that the previous king, Richard II, had wanted Mortimer to be the next king. Worcester and Northumberland helped Henry become king, and they find that they are now accused of murdering

Richard II. For all their loyalty to Henry, he hasn't been loyal to them. They unfold a plot to depose King Henry—to remove him from the throne.

This is the end of Act I. Act II begins outside a tavern on a dark road between London and Canterbury. One of Falstaff's tavern buddies encounters a servant who tells them he has already run into one of the rich travelers they plan to rob.

ACT II
Scene 1

Outside a tavern on the road between London and Canterbury.

(ENTER SERVANT from one side and TAVERN MATE from the other side.)

TAVERN MATE:

What ho, you, servant!

SERVANT:

Good morrow, Master. As I told you yesternight, there's a farmer from Kent here who hath brought with him 300 marks in gold. I heard him tell it to one of his company last night at supper. They are up already, calling for eggs and butter.

TAVERN MATE:

Sirrah, they will meet with thieves—of that we will make sure, or you will have this neck.

(EXIT.)

ACT II
Scene 2

NARRATOR:

In the sixteenth century, all sorts of people made religious pilgrimages to the cathedral at Canterbury. Rich people took their horses, poor people walked, and most people carried whatever money they had with them. Thieves knew this. In this scene Falstaff and his drinking mate prepare to rob the travelers, and Shakespeare makes them look like buffoons. When Prince Hal and his friend Poins carry out their plan and steal the stolen money from Falstaff, Shakespeare's audience would have been howling with delight.

(ENTER FALSTAFF.)

FALSTAFF:

Poins! Poins! My horse, you rogue!

(POINS ENTERS but Falstaff should not see him. He should be pretending to lead Falstaff's horse away. Or Poins can simply cross the stage and EXIT again. Meanwhile PRINCE HAL ENTERS.)

PRINCE HAL:

Peace, you fat-kidneyed rascal!

FALSTAFF:

Hal, that rascal Poins has hid my horse and I know not where. For me, eight yards of uneven ground is threescore and ten miles on foot, and they know it! A plague when thieves can't be true to one another!

PRINCE:

Peace, you fat-guts! Lie down. Lay thy ear to the ground and listen to hear the tread of the travelers.

FALSTAFF:

Lie down? And do you have any levers to lift me up again? I pray thee, Prince Hal, lead me to my horse.

PRINCE:

Out, you rogue! Am I your servant?

FALSTAFF:

Go hang thyself in thine own heir-apparent garters!

(ENTER TAVERN MATES. RE-ENTER POINS.)

TAVERN MATE:

Stand!

FALSTAFF:

So I do, against my will.

TAVERN MATE:

There's men with money of the king's, coming down the hill, going to the king's exchequer.

SECOND TAVERN MATE:

How many be there of them?

TAVERN MATE:

Some eight or ten.

FALSTAFF:

Zounds, will they not rob us?

PRINCE:

What? A coward, Sir John Paunch?
(To Poins.) Where are our disguises?

POINS:

Here, hard by. Stand close.

(ENTER TRAVELERS carrying purses or sacks.)

TRAVELER 1:

Come, neighbor. The boy shall lead our horses down the hill; we'll walk awhile and ease our legs.

(Falstaff and the others jump them.)

TRAVELER 2:

Bless us!

TRAVELER 1:

Oh, we are undone, both we and ours forever!

(Falstaff and the others rob them and bind them. EXIT.)

(ENTER PRINCE and POINS, masked.)

PRINCE:

The thieves have bound the true men. Now you and I rob the thieves and go merrily to London.

POINS:

I hear them coming!

(ENTER FALSTAFF and TAVERN MATES. Poins and Prince Hal stand back so Falstaff and the others don't see them. All of a sudden the Prince and Poins jump out at them.)

PRINCE:

(Voice disguised.)
Your money!

POINS:

Villains!

(Prince and Poins rob TAVERN MATES, who then drop the loot and EXIT.)

PRINCE:

Poor Falstaff! Were it not for laughing, I should pity him!

(Pick up purses or bags and EXIT.)

ACT II
Scene 3

Hotspur's castle.

NARRATOR:

Meanwhile Hotspur prepares to go to battle again. This scene shows Hotspur at home with his wife Lady Percy, whom he calls Kate. Hotspur is reading a letter he received from an adviser who thinks his campaign is a bad idea. Hotspur is always ready to ride off for another glorious moment on the battlefield, and Kate is getting a little tired of this.

(ENTER HOTSPUR, reading a letter.)

HOTSPUR:

(Reading aloud.)

". . . The purpose you undertake is dangerous, the friends you have named uncertain, the time itself unsorted, and your whole plot too light for so great an opposition."

Oh yes? Say you so? Well, you are shallow and cowardly and you lie.

(ENTER LADY PERCY/KATE.)

KATE:

O my good lord, why are you thus alone?
Tell me, sweet lord, what is it that takes from thee
Thy appetite and thy golden sleep?
In thy faint slumbers I hear murmurs of iron wars,
And cries of "Courage!" and "To the field!"
Some heavy business hath my lord in hand,
And I must know it, else he loves me not.

(ENTER SERVANT.)

HOTSPUR:

Have you my horse?

SERVANT:

Ay, my lord.

KATE:

My dear husband, what is it that carries you away?

HOTSPUR:

Why my horse, my love—my horse carries me away!

KATE:

Out, you mad-headed ape!
Answer me directly or I'll break thy little finger, Harry!

HOTSPUR:

Away, away! I love thee not! This is no world
To play with dolls and dabble with love.
We must have bloody noses and cracked crowns.

KATE:

You do not love me? You do not indeed?

HOTSPUR:

Come, will you see me ride?
When I am on horseback, I will say
I love you forever. But hark, Kate *(Softening, sounding nicer.)*
You must not question me about where I go or the reason I go.
This evening I leave you, gentle Kate.
You are good and trustworthy.
But you cannot tell what you do not know,
And so far will I trust thee.

KATE:

You will trust me only so far?

HOTSPUR:

Not an inch further. But listen, Kate—hark.
Whither I go today, tomorrow you will go.
Will this content you?

KATE:

It must.

(EXIT HOTSPUR and KATE.)

ACT II
Scene 4

The tavern.

NARRATOR:

Now we get back to Prince Hal and Poins, waiting in the London tavern for Falstaff and his buddy to show up. When they do, they are full of bragging for having beaten off a dozen men they claim attacked them.

(ENTER POINS and PRINCE HAL.)

PRINCE:

Sirrah, Falstaff and the rest of the thieves are at the door. Shall we be merry?

POINS:

As merry as crickets, my lad.

PRINCE:

I pray thee, call in Falstaff. Call in ribs, call in tallow!

(ENTER FALSTAFF and TAVERN MATE.)

FALSTAFF:

A plague of all cowards, I say! Amen! Give me a cup of sack, boy. Is there no virtue anymore? *(He tastes, makes a face, spits it out.)*

(Prince and Poins laugh heartily.)

FALSTAFF:

There is lime powder in this sack! Why, there is nothing but mischief to be found in villainous men. A plague of all cowards, I say still!

PRINCE:

How now, woolsack? What mutter you?

FALSTAFF:

Are not you a coward? And Poins there? I am a rogue if I have not fought with a dozen men two hours together. I have escaped by a miracle.

TAVERN MATE:

We set upon some dozen—

FALSTAFF:

Sixteen at least, my lord.

TAVERN MATE:

And bound them. Then six or seven fresh men set upon us—

FALSTAFF:

And unbound the rest, and then come in the other.

PRINCE:

What, fought you with them all?

FALSTAFF:

I know not what you call *all*, but if I fought not with fifty of them, I am a bunch of radish!

PRINCE:

Pray God you have not murdered some of them.

FALSTAFF:

Nay, that's past praying for. I have peppered two of them, I am sure, two rogues in buckram suits. I tell thee what, Hal—if I tell thee a lie, spit in my face, call me horse. Here's my point. Four rogues in buckram let drive at me.

PRINCE:

What, four? Thou said but two just now.

FALSTAFF:

Four, Hal. I told thee four.

POINS:

Ay, ay, he said four.

FALSTAFF:

These four came at me, but I made no more ado but took all their seven points in my target—thus.

PRINCE:

Seven? Why, there were but four even now.

FALSTAFF:

These nine men in buckram I have told thee of—

PRINCE:

So . . . two more already.

FALSTAFF:

Their points being broken— *(Interrupted by Poins, starting to laugh.)* — they began to give me ground, but I followed close. Seven of the eleven I struck.

PRINCE:

O monstrous! Eleven buckram men grown out of two! Why, these lies are monstrous, like the father who begets them! Thou clay-brained guts, thou knotty-pated fool— We *two* saw you *four* set on *four* travelers, and bind them, and become masters of their wealth. Then we *two* set on you *four* and outfaced you from your prize. What a coward you are to hack thy sword in two and say it was in fight!

FALSTAFF:

(Quickly thinking up a different angle.) By my Lord, I knew ye! I could not turn upon the true prince, now could I? Ah well, I was a coward but on instinct! The lion will not touch the true prince. I for a valiant lion, and thou for a true prince! Come, shall we be merry? Gallants, lads, boys, hearts of gold—

(ENTER MISTRESS QUICKLY, the tavern hostess.)

MISTRESS QUICKLY:

Oh! My lord the prince! There is a noble man of the court at the door to speak with you. He says he comes from your father.

PRINCE:

Send him back again to my mother.

FALSTAFF:

Shall I give him his answer?

PRINCE:

Pray thee do, Jack.

(EXIT ALL.)

NARRATOR:

A man has come from the king's court to tell the prince there is villainous news from home and that he must return immediately. He reports that Hotspur has betrayed his loyalty to the king and is allying himself with Scotland. Prince Hal doesn't seem to quite grasp the seriousness of this news. But Falstaff tells him he'd better practice talking to his father, so they put on a humorous skit for each other.

(ENTER MISTRESS QUICKLY, FALSTAFF, and PRINCE HAL)

FALSTAFF:

Your father's beard has turned white with the news—there are a thousand Scottish soldiers, and you may buy land now as cheap as stinking mackerel. As heir apparent, could the world pick out three such enemies as that fiend Douglas the Scot, that spirit Percy the Hotspur, and Glendower the devil? Are you not horribly afraid? Does not thy blood thrill at it?

PRINCE:

Not a whit, in faith. I lack some of your instinct.

FALSTAFF:

Then you will be horribly chided tomorrow when you come before your father. Come, practice your answer.

PRINCE:

Do stand for my father and examine me upon the particulars of my life.

FALSTAFF:

Shall I? This chair shall be my state, this dagger my scepter, and this cushion my crown.

PRINCE:

(Bowing.) Well, here is my leg.

FALSTAFF:

And here is my speech . . .

MISTRESS QUICKLY:

(Laughing.) Oh, this is excellent sport!
Look how he holds his countenance as the Father!

FALSTAFF:

(Falstaff pretends to be the king.)

Harry, I marvel at where thou spendest thy time and how thou art accompanied. Youth, the more it is wasted, the sooner it wears out. Shall the son of England prove a thief and take purses? A question to be asked . . . And yet, there is a virtuous man I have often noted in thy company, but I know not his name.

PRINCE:

What manner of man is he, your majesty?

FALSTAFF:

A good, portly man, of a cheerful look, a pleasing eye, and a most noble carriage. Now I remember me, his name is Falstaff. I speak the truth—there is virtue in that Falstaff. Now, tell me: Where hast thou been this month?

PRINCE:

Now you stand for me and I'll play my father.

(They switch places.)

PRINCE:

Now Harry, the complaints I hear of you are grievous. There is a devil haunts you in the likeness of an old fat man. Why do you converse with that trunk of humors, that bolting hutch of beastliness—what is he good for?

FALSTAFF:

Whom means your grace?

PRINCE:

That villainous abominable misleader of youth—
Falstaff—that old, white-bearded Satan.

FALSTAFF:

My lord, I know the man. But to say I know more harm in him than in myself, were to say more than I know. Yes he is old—more is the pity. But if sack and sugar are a fault, God help the wicked! If to be fat is to be hated, then Pharoah's lean kin are to be loved. No, my good lord. Banish all the rest, but for sweet Jack Falstaff, kind Jack Falstaff, true Jack Falstaff, valiant Jack Falstaff, banish not him thy Harry's company. Banish plump Jack, and banish all the world!

PRINCE:

I do, I will.

(Knocking heard. MISTRESS QUICKLY EXITS, then RE-ENTERS.)

MISTRESS QUICKLY:

The sheriff and all the watch are at the door. They are come to search the house. Shall I let them in?

PRINCE:

(To Falstaff.) Go! Hide!

(ENTER SHERIFF and SERVANT.)

SHERIFF:

First, pardon me, my lord. A complaint has followed certain men to this house.

PRINCE:

What men?

SHERIFF:

One of them is well known, my gracious lord—a large man.

SERVANT:

As fat as butter.

SHERIFF:

There are two gentlemen, my lord,
Who have been robbed of three hundred marks.

PRINCE:

The man, I assure you, is not here. By tomorrow dinnertime
I will send him to answer you.
If he has robbed these men he shall be answerable.

SHERIFF:

And now we will leave this house. Good night, my noble lord.

(SHERIFF and MISTRESS QUICKLY EXIT.)

(Prince goes to alert Falstaff and finds him asleep. He checks his pockets, find some old papers, which he reads.)

PRINCE:

Search his pockets. What do you find?

SERVANT:

Nothing but papers, my lord. Some bills from the tavern.
(Hands papers to Prince Hal.)

PRINCE:

Let me read these bills and papers. *(Sorts through them.)* Oh, monstrous! Such an intolerable amount of drink. Whatever else there is, we'll read later. Let him sleep there 'til day. I will go to court in the morning and see my father. We must go to the wars. I will get for this villain the command of some foot soldiers. Be with me early in the morning. Good morrow.

SERVANT:

Good morrow, good my lord.

(THEY EXIT.)

ACT III
Scene 1

Wales, outside Glendower's caste.

NARRATOR:

In Act III, the rebellion really begins to heat up. Hotspur and the other rebels are in Wales now, firming up their plot against King Henry. At this point, they are confident that their rebellion will succeed, but they are already squabbling with each other about dividing up the new kingdom. There is a lot of friction between Hotspur and the wild Welshman Glendower, who is related to him by marriage.

(ENTER HOTSPUR, WORCESTER, GLENDOWER, and MORTIMER.)

HOTSPUR:

So? Shall we be gone?

GLENDOWER:

The moon shines fair; you may away by night.
I'll break the news of your departure to your wives.
I am afraid my daughter will run mad.
So much she dotes on her Mortimer.

(Puts his hand on Mortimer's shoulder.)

(EXIT GLENDOWER.)

MORTIMER:

Fie, cousin Percy! How you cross my wife's father!

HOTSPUR:

O, he is as tedious as a tired horse, a railing wife;
Worse than a smoky house. I had rather live
With cheese and garlic in a windmill far
Than feed on sweets and have him talk to me.

MORTIMER:

In faith, he is a worthy gentleman,
But few men could cross him as you have done.

WORCESTER:

Sir, you put him quite besides his patience.
You must learn to amend this fault.

HOTSPUR:

(Sarcastically.) Well, well, I am schooled. Good manners be your speed!
Here come our wives, and let us take our leave.

(ENTER GLENDOWER with Hotspur's wife KATE and MORTIMER'S WIFE.)

MORTIMER:

This is what vexes me—
My wife can speak no English, I no Welsh.

GLENDOWER:

My daughter weeps; she will not part with you;
She wishes she were a soldier too, and would go to the wars.

(Pantomime scene with MUSIC. Mortimer and his wife act out a reluctant good-bye scene with much weeping and wailing by Mortimer's wife—but not Hotspur's wife. Lady Mortimer must hum or sing as if in another language. Meanwhile, Kate stands by with her arms folded, smiling mockingly.)

HOTSPUR:

Come, Kate, I'll have your song too.

KATE:

Not mine, for sure! I will not sing.

GLENDOWER:

Come, come, Lord Mortimer. You are as slow
As hot Lord Percy is on fire to go.
And then to horse immediately.

King Henry IV,
Part I

MORTIMER:

With all my heart.

(EXIT ALL.)

ACT III
Scene 2

King's castle.

NARRATOR:

The time has come for the king and his son to meet with each other, and it seems that Hal is beginning to take his role as Prince seriously.

(ENTER KING HENRY and PRINCE HAL)

KING:

Harry, my son.
You are too often in vile company.
You have therefore lost your princely privilege and
Every eye is weary of thy sight—
Except mine, which desires to see thee more.

PRINCE:

I shall hereafter, my thrice-gracious lord,
Be more myself.

KING:

The peace and safety of our throne is shaken.
Are you likely to fight against me under Hotspur's pay
To dog his heels and curtsy at his frowns
And show me how much you are degenerate?

PRINCE:

Do not think so. You shall not find it so.
I will redeem all this on Percy's head
And, in the closing of some glorious day,
Be bold to tell you that I am your son.

(ENTER MESSENGER.).

KING:

How now, good man?

MESSENGER:

Douglas and the English rebels met
At Shrewsbury, Your Majesty—
A mighty and fearful force they are.

KING:

This news is five days old.
Harry, you shall set out Wednesday next and
Thursday we ourselves will march.
Our hands are full of business. Let's away!
Advantage feeds him fat while men delay.

(EXIT ALL.)

ACT III
Scene 3

The tavern.

NARRATOR:

Prince Hal readies himself to go to war to defend his father's honor and
ward off those who would overthrow his rule. Meanwhile, back at the tavern,
Falstaff confronts Mistress Quickly.

(ENTER FALSTAFF and MISTRESS QUICKLY.)

FALSTAFF:

Have you enquired yet who picked my pocket?

MISTRESS QUICKLY:

Why, Sir John, what do you think? Do you think I keep thieves in my house? You owe me money, besides, for your diet and drinkings between meals.

(ENTER PRINCE.)

FALSTAFF:

Hal! The other night I fell asleep here and had my pocket picked. I lost three or four bonds of forty pounds apiece and a seal ring of my grandfather's.

PRINCE:

Why, you impudent rascal! There was nothing in your pockets but tavern bills and one poor pennyworth of sugar candy. Are you not ashamed to charge an honest woman with picking thy pocket?

FALSTAFF:

Hostess, I forgive thee. Go make ready breakfast, woman.
(Pompously and grandly, as if giving a speech.) Love thy husband, look to thy servants, cherish thy guests.

(EXIT MISTRESS QUICKLY, throwing up her hands in disgust.)

FALSTAFF:

Now, Hal. The news at court. For the robbery, lad—how is that answered?

PRINCE:

O my sweet beef, I must still be good angel to thee. The money is paid back. And I have procured you a charge of foot soldiers.

FALSTAFF:

I wish it were on horse. Well, God be thanked for these rebels.

(EXIT FALSTAFF and PRINCE.)

NARRATOR:

The prince is growing up fast. Prince Hal is getting impatient with his friend for lying about what was stolen from his pockets and for treating the tavern hostess badly. But the prince is still loyal to Falstaff. He has repaid the money from the robbery of the travelers, and he has also gotten Falstaff the command of an infantry unit in the battle that's coming up. Falstaff sees the war as a chance to make himself look good.

ACT IV
Scene 1

Battlefield.

NARRATOR:

The rebellion is not going well for Hotspur and the rebel forces. Hotspur's father, Lord Northumberland, is sick and has sent word that they should go on without him. Meanwhile, news is reaching the rebels that the King's forces are much, much stronger than they thought.

(ENTER HOTSPUR, DOUGLAS THE SCOT, and VERNON.)

HOTSPUR:

Douglas, my noble Scot. A braver place
In my heart has no man but yourself.

DOUGLAS:

(Bowing.) Thou art the king of honor.

VERNON:

Sir—the Earl of Westmoreland, seven thousand strong
Is marching this way, and with him Prince John.
The king himself is set forth
With strong an might preparation.

HOTSPUR:

He shall be welcome. And where is his son
The nimble-footed madcap, Prince of Wales?

VERNON:

All furnished, all in arms;
All plumed like ostriches
And glittering in golden coats,
As full of spirit as the month of May
And gorgeous as the sun at midsummer.

HOTSPUR:

No more, no more!
Harry to Harry shall meet, horse to horse
And never part 'till one drops down a corpse.
Oh, I wish Glendower would come!

VERNON:

There is more news.
Glendower has not drawn his forces together
These fourteen days.

HOTSPUR:

What may the king's whole army reach unto?

VERNON:

To thirty thousand.

HOTSPUR:

Let it be forty.
Doomsday is near. Die all, die merrily.

(EXIT ALL.)

ACT IV
Scene 2

NARRATOR:

As the rebel forces are arguing with each other about when and how to attack, Sir Walter Blunt arrives with a peace offering from the king.

(ENTER HOTSPUR, WORCESTER, and DOUGLAS.)

HOTSPUR:

We'll fight with him tonight.

WORCESTER:

It may not be.

HOTSPUR:

Tonight, say I—

(ENTER Sir Walter Blunt.)

HOTSPUR:

Welcome! You come from the king.

BLUNT:

The king asks that you name your griefs
And wishes to grant you absolute pardon for yourself
And those you have misled.

HOTSPUR:

The king is kind and well we know the king
Knows when to promise, when to pay.
But he has broken oath on oath.
He has committed wrong on wrong.
We are driven to pry into his right to his title
Which we think he should not keep.

BLUNT:

Shall I return this answer to the king?

HOTSPUR:

Not so, sir. We'll withdraw awhile.
Go to the king; receive for us
Some guarantee of our safe return.
In the morning early shall my uncle
Bring him our purposes. Farewell.

BLUNT:

I would you would accept his grace and love.

HOTSPUR:

And may be so we shall.

BLUNT:

Pray God you do.

(EXIT ALL but Narrator.)

NARRATOR:

The king does want to make peace, and Hotspur knows that he and his rebel soldiers are far outnumbered by the king's forces. He sees that it would be better to accept the king's outstretched hand. He plans to send his uncle Worcester to talk with the king in the morning.

ACT V
Scene 1

King's court.

(ENTER KING, PRINCE HAL, PRINCE JOHN, and FALSTAFF.)

KING:

How bloodily the sun begins to appear
Above yonder hill! The day looks pale.

PRINCE:

It foretells a tempest storm and a blustering day.

KING:

How now, my Lord of Worcester? 'Tis not well

That you and I shall meet. You have deceived our trust.

What say you? Will you unknit

This knot of hated war?

WORCESTER:

I do protest, my lord. I have not sought the day of this dislike.

KING:

You have not sought it! How comes it then?

FALSTAFF:

Rebellion lay in his way and he found it.

PRINCE:

Peace, chewet, peace!

WORCESTER:

I must remember you, my lord.

We were the first and dearest of your friends.

But in short space

Fortune rained down on your head

And such a flood of greatness fell on you.

You forgot your oath to us.

You used us as that ungentle gull, the cuckoo's bird

Uses the sparrow.

KING:

These things you have

Proclaimed at markets and read in churches.

You use thin colors to paint the cause of your rebellion.

PRINCE:

In both your armies there are many

Who shall pay dearly for this encounter.

Tell your nephew I praise his valor

And to save the blood on either side

Will try fortune with him in a single fight.

KING:

We love our people well, even those
Who are misled. Every man shall be my friend again.
But if he will not yield
Rebuke and dreaded conflict wait upon us.
Be gone, good Worcester.
We offer fair; take it advisedly.

(EXIT WORCESTER, followed by PRINCE JOHN and KING.)

NARRATOR:

Falstaff is preparing to lead his army into battle—but it is not the army Prince Hal assigned to him. Falstaff has pulled a fast one. He took money from his foot soldiers and used part of it to pay other beggars, prisoners, and other desperate men willing to risk their lives for a few coins.

PRINCE HAL:

(To Falstaff.) Say thy prayers and farewell.

FALSTAFF:

I would 'twere bedtime, Hal, and all well.

PRINCE:

Why, thou owest God a death.

(EXIT PRINCE. Falstaff looks sad, shakes his head, moves forward onstage.)

NARRATOR:

Falstaff may be a comic character in this play, but often in Shakespeare the truth is spoken by someone other than the play's hero. Falstaff knows that many people on both sides are about to die, and he asks the question many people ask: Is there really honor in dying for a cause? Where is the honor when you are dead?

FALSTAFF:

My death is not due yet. I would not pay before my time . . . well, no matter. Honor spurs me on. But what if honor kills me off after it spurs me on? Can honor set a broken leg? Or an arm? No. Or take away the grief of a wound? No, honor has no skill in surgery. What is honor then? A word. Can he that died on Wednesday feel it? No. Can he hear it? No. Honor is a mere burying cloth. I'll have none of it.

(FALSTAFF EXITS.)

ACT V
Scene 2

(ENTER WORCESTER and VERNON.)

WORCESTER:

O no, my nephew must not know, Sir Richard,
The liberal and kind offer of the king.

VERNON:

'Twere best he did.

WORCESTER:

It is not possible the king shall keep his word in loving us.

(ENTER HOTSPUR.)

HOTSPUR:

Uncle, what news?

WORCESTER:

There is no mercy in the king.

HOTSPUR:

Did you beg any? God forbid!

WORCESTER:

I told him gently of our grievances.
He calls us rebels, traitors—

(ENTER DOUGLAS.)

DOUGLAS:

Arms, Gentlemen! To arms!
I have sent a proud defiance to the king
Which will surely bring him quickly on.

WORCESTER:

The Prince of Wales stepped before the king
And challenged you to single fight.

HOTSPUR:

O, if only the quarrel lay on our heads alone!
Was his challenge in contempt?

VERNON:

No, by my soul.

He urged the challenge modestly.

He trimmed up your praises with a princely tongue.

MESSENGER:

My lord, prepare. The king comes on apace.

HOTSPUR:

Gentleman, the time of life is short!

Now, Hope! Set on!

Sound all the lofty instruments of war

And by that music let us all now embrace;

For some of us never shall a second time.

(Hotspur, Douglas embrace. Optional: TRUMPETS SOUND. EXIT.).

NARRATOR:

Hotspur is afraid now—afraid for his men, afraid for his own life. If only Worcester had told him the truth—that the king intended to make peace, Hotspur would gladly have accepted it.

ACT V
Scene 3

(KING MARCHES ACROSS STAGE WITH HIS MEN. TRUMPETS SOUND. EXIT, marching.)

(Body lying onstage in a coat or cape like the king's.)

(ENTER DOUGLAS and HOTSPUR.)

DOUGLAS:

All's done, all's won. Here breathless lies the king!

HOTSPUR:

Where?

DOUGLAS:

Here.

HOTSPUR:

This, Douglas? No. I know this face full well.

A gallant knight he was, but not the king.

He is dressed to look like the king himself.

DOUGLAS:

(To the dead man.) A fool goes with thy soul!
Why didst thou tell me thou wert a king?

HOTSPUR:

The king has many marching in his coats.

DOUGLAS:

Now, by my sword, I will kill all his coats;
I'll murder all his wardrobe, piece by piece
Until I meet the king.

(HOTSPUR and DOUGLAS EXIT.)

(ENTER FALSTAFF.)

FALSTAFF:

Soft! Who are you? There's honor for you. God, keep lead out of me. I have led my rag-of-muffin soldiers where they are peppered. There's not three of my hundred and fifty alive.

(ENTER PRINCE.)

PRINCE:

What, you stand here idle? Lend me thy sword.

FALSTAFF:

O Hal, I pray thee give me leave to breathe awhile. Great heroes never did such deeds as I have done this day. I have paid Percy; I have made him sure.

PRINCE:

He is sure indeed, and living to kill thee.
I pray thee, lend me thy sword.

FALSTAFF:

Nay, before God, Hal, if Hotspur is alive, you get not my sword, but take my pistol.

PRINCE:

Give it me. What, is it in the case?
(Prince pulls it out and finds it's a bottle. He throws the bottle at Falstaff in disgust.)
What, is it time to jest and dally now?

(EXIT.)

ACT V
Scene 3

(ALARM SOUNDS. ENTER KING, PRINCE, LORD JOHN, and WESTMORELAND.)

KING:

I pray thee, Harry, withdraw thyself. Thou bleedest too much.
Lord John, go with your brother.

JOHN:

Not I, my lord, unless I did bleed too.
 Come, cousin Westmoreland, our duty this way lies.

(EXIT JOHN and WESTMORELAND.)

(ENTER DOUGLAS.)

DOUGLAS:

Another king? They grow like Hydra's heads.
I am *the* Douglas, fatal to all those
Who wear those colors on them. What art thou
That counterfeits the person of a king?

KING:

I am the king himself.

(They start to fight. ENTER PRINCE OF WALES, who fights Douglas, and DOUGLAS FLEES offstage.)

PRINCE:

Look cheerily, my lord. How fares your grace?

KING:

Stay and breathe awhile.
You have rescued me.

(EXIT KING.)

(ENTER HOTSPUR.)

HOTSPUR:

If I mistake not, thou art Prince Hal.

PRINCE:

You speak as if I would deny my name.

HOTSPUR:

My name is Harry Percy. I am Hotspur.

PRINCE:

I am the Prince of Wales, and think not, Percy,
To share with me in glory any more.
Two stars keep not their motion in one sphere,
Nor can one England have a double reign
Of Harry Percy and the Prince of Wales.

(They fight. ENTER FALSTAFF.)

(ENTER DOUGLAS. Douglas fights with Falstaff, who falls down as if dead. EXIT DOUGLAS.)

(Hotspur falls.)

HOTSPUR:

(Gasping for breath.)
O Harry, thou hast robbed me of my youth!
No, Percy, thou art dust and food for—

PRINCE:

For worms, brave Percy. You are food for worms.
Fare thee well, great heart.

(Hotspur dies.)

(Prince sees Falstaff lying on the ground and thinks he is dead.)

PRINCE:

What, old acquaintance? Could not all this flesh
Keep in a little life?
O, I should have a heavy miss of thee
If I were much in love with vanity.
Emboweled will I see thee by and by;
Till then in blood by noble Percy lie.

(EXIT PRINCE. Falstaff gets up.)

FALSTAFF:

Emboweled? If thou embowel me today, I'll give you leave to powder me and eat me tomorrow. No, it was time to counterfeit. The better part of valor is discretion, in which better part I have saved my life. *(Falstaff examines the dead Hotspur.)* I am afraid he might prove the better counterfeit.

Therefore, I'll make him sure, yea, and I'll swear I killed him myself.
(*Stabs him. Takes up Hotspur and drags him.*)

(*ENTER PRINCE and his brother LORD JOHN.*)

JOHN:

Whom have we here? Did you not tell me this fat man was dead?

PRINCE:

I did; I saw him dead,
Breathless and bleeding on the ground. Art thou alive?
Or is it fantasy?

FALSTAFF:

I am not a double man, but if I be not Jack Falstaff, then am I a fool. If your father will do me any honor, good. If not, let him kill the next Percy himself.

PRINCE:

Why, Percy I killed myself, and saw thee dead!

FALSTAFF:

Did you? Lord, Lord, how this world is given to lying. I grant you I was down and out of breath, and so was he. But we both rose at an instant and fought a long hour by Shrewsbury clock.

JOHN:

This is the strangest tale that ever I heard.

PRINCE:

This is the strangest fellow, brother John.
Come, Jack Falstaff, carry your luggage nobly on your back.
If a lie may do thee credit,
I'll gild it with the happiest terms I have.

(*EXIT.*)

ACT V
Scene 4

NARRATOR:

As you will see in the last scene of our play, the business of this war is not yet over. Prince Hal has shown himself to be a fine warrior and a gracious friend. In talking to his father, he does not even take credit for slaying Hotspur.

(ENTER KING, PRINCE, WESTMORELAND, JOHN, and a GUARD holding WORCESTER by the arm.)

KING:

Thus ever did rebellion find rebuke.

You, ill-spirited Worcester, did not we send grace,

Pardon, and terms of love to all of you?

WORCESTER:

What I have done my safety urged me to.

KING:

Bear Worcester to the death.

(EXIT WORCESTER with GUARD.)

KING:

How goes the field?

PRINCE:

The noble Scot, Lord Douglas, has fled

When he saw the fortune of the day turned from him, and

The noble Hotspur is slain.

The pursuers took him and at my tent

The noble Douglas is.

KING:

Then this remains,

That we divide our power.

(King straightens up to deliver final four lines forcefully.)

Rebellion in this land shall lose its sway,

Meeting the check of another day.

And so this business so fair is done;

Let us not leave till all our own be won.

(EXIT ALL.)

(MUSIC.)

Twelfth Night

Malvolio resplendent in crossed garters and a Pilgrim's hat.

This costume shows how one character might embody more than one quality:
Malvolio has a Puritanical streak, which makes him irresistible to tricksters.

Twelfth Night is one of Shakespeare's best-loved comedies, with many of his standard comic elements: a girl dressed as a boy, a major practical joke on a foolish character, a fool who tells the truth, two cases of unrequited love, and everything coming up roses in the end. It is believed to have been written in late 1600, to be performed for Queen Elizabeth on Twelfth Night (January 6), a traditional night of merry-making.

The play opens with a petulant Orsino, Duke of Illyria, commanding his court musicians to "play on!" Just as quickly he decides he has had "enough!" Lady Olivia has rejected his love, and music cannot console him. In the next scene, we meet Viola, who has just landed on the island of Illyria when a boat carrying her and her twin brother Sebastian was wrecked. She thinks he is lost forever when she loses track of him in the raging sea. She makes the best of it by dressing herself as a young man, calling herself Cesario, and becoming Duke Orsino's page. Now the trouble starts.

Children do a fantastic job with this play. They really enjoy portraying the comic characters—Sir Toby Belch, Sir Andrew Aguecheek, and Malvolio. But the straight characters are also rewarding roles. Duke Orsino has nothing to do but pine away for the lovely Lady Olivia. The feisty Maria loves scolding her friends Sir Toby and Sir Andrew and letting them in on her idea for tricking the pompous servant Malvolio. Viola is a plucky young girl who can scarcely maintain her composure—or her pretense of being the boy Cesario—when she finds herself falling in love with the duke. Viola's twin brother Sebastian is bewildered when he finds himself mistaken for Cesario, but he is only too happy to marry the lovely Lady Olivia when she asks him. Feste the Clown makes about as much sense as anyone when he dances alone on the stage at the end of the last act. He sings (or is accompanied by a recording of) the famous madrigal "When that I was and a little tiny boy/ With hey, ho, the wind and the rain/ A foolish thing was but a toy/ For the rain it raineth every day."

In this play, as in all these children's productions, costumes should not be elaborate. But do try to find some yellow tights, leggings, or pants for Malvolio and wind red ribbons around his legs for the crossed garters. The poor guy has been convinced by a forged letter that Olivia—the lady he serves—is in love with him and "bids him to come before her all smiling and cross-gartered, in yellow stockings." When Malvolio walks onstage in this garb, allow time for laughter to subside!

One last word on the comedy. *Twelfth Night* has plenty of silly scenes, which children love. However, it is not cruel and it is not stupid. Unlike many comedies by lesser playwrights, the real thing never dips down into bad taste or slapstick.

Suggested Music

Songs & Dances from Shakespeare (compact disc). The Broadside Band, Saydisc Records, 1994.

Come, Gentle Night: Music of Shakespeare's World (compact disc), tracks 3, 20, 27, 31, 39. Ensemble Galilei, Telarc Records, 2000.

Other suggestions for music: live or recorded music of any type, but especially madrigals and Renaissance songs.

Note: There are several famous songs associated with this play. The track numbers I've cited indicate these. The song "When That I Was and a Little Tiny Boy," which Feste the Clown dances to at the end of the play, is very traditional in productions of *Twelfth Night*.

Suggested Props

Blanket and pillows
Fruit
Musical instruments
Mugs
Table
Ring
Change purse
Letter
Jewel or pearl
Swords for duel (two)

Suggested Backdrops

Ocean
Elegant room
Countryside

Suggested Costumes

Gentlemen should wear leggings and tunics (shirts or blouses), but Duke Orsino should look grander than the other men. (Add a silkier shirt or a long cape.) Hats for Sir Andrew and Sir Toby would be a nice touch. Similarly, Lady Olivia should have a fancier gown than Maria. Viola should wear a simple dress when she is appearing as herself and young man's clothes that are the same as Sebastian's when she is pretending to be Cesario. Feste the Clown can have any offbeat combination of clothes—don't be limited by traditional "clown" garb. Malvolio must have yellow stockings or leggings and criss-crossed garters (ribbons wound around his legs) for his scene in the third act.

Cast of Characters

Orsino, Duke of Illyria

Sebastian, brother of Viola

Antonio, a sea captain and friend of Sebastian

Sea captain, friend of Viola

Valentine, gentleman attending the duke

Sir Toby Belch, Olivia's uncle

Sir Andrew Aguecheek

Malvolio, steward to Olivia

Feste, clown and servant to Olivia

Olivia, a countess

Viola, sister of Sebastian

Maria, attendant to Olivia

Duke's officers (one or two)

Musicians and attendants to Duke Orsino and Olivia (if available)

Priest

Sailors, officers, musicians, and servants as needed

Pronunciation Guide to Names

Aguecheek (ay-gyoo-cheek)

Cesario (say-zar-ee-oh)

Curio (kyoor-ee-oh)

Fabian (fay-bee-uhn)

Feste (fess-tay)

Malvolio (mal-voh-lee-oh)

Maria (mar-iyh-uh *or* mar-ee-uh)

Orsino (or-see-noh)

Topas (toh-pus)

Scenes

Duke's palace, beach, Olivia's house, and a street in town.

Twelfth Night

ACT 1
Scene 1

Duke's palace.

(ENTER NARRATOR, ORSINO, CURIO, and other LORDS or MUSICIANS [optional].)

(MUSIC.)

(Characters strike poses of thoughtful attention to the music or, if there are any, to the onstage musicians.)

NARRATOR:

Ladies and gentleman, kindred spirits, and all lovers of love attend! Welcome to our play *Twelfth Night*, a delightful comedy written by our friend Mr. William Shakespeare around the year 1601. You will see before you on the stage Duke Orsino, a sensitive and good duke of the country of Illyria, and his men. The duke is in love with the lady Olivia, but alas she does not love him. She has told him that because of her grief over the death of her brother, she will remain veiled and shut up in her house and will admit no one until seven years have passed.

DUKE ORSINO:

If music be the food of love, play on
Give me too much of it . . . oh
Enough! No more!
'Tis not so sweet now as it was before.

(ENTER VALENTINE.)

DUKE ORSINO:

How now? What news from her?

VALENTINE:

So please my lord, I was not admitted.
But from her handmaid do return this answer,
That no one shall behold her face
For seven long years. That's how long she would honor
Her dead brother's love,
And keep his memory fresh and lasting.

DUKE ORSINO:

Oh, if she loves a brother so now,

How she will love when Cupid's arrow

Rids her of all other affections!

Away before me to sweet beds of flowers!

Love thoughts lie rich when canopied with bowers.

(EXIT DUKE, CURIO, and VALENTINE.)

(Sound of waves breaking on shore and/or actors can wave blue silky fabric to represent water.)

ACT I
Scene 2

Seacoast or beach.

NARRATOR:

While Orsino tries to convince himself that one day Olivia will love him, another situation is unfolding in our play. A young woman named Viola and her twin brother Sebastian have been shipwrecked off the coast of Illyria.

Viola, the captain of the boat, and a few of the sailors are safe, but her brother Sebastian is gone, and Viola is afraid he has drowned. The captain comforts her by telling her that he last saw Sebastian clinging to a piece of the ship's mast, so there is a good chance he has survived.

(ENTER VIOLA and SEA CAPTAIN.)

VIOLA:

What country, friends, is this?

CAPTAIN:

This is Illyria, lady.

VIOLA:

And what should I do in Illyria?

Oh, sailors, do you think my brother Sebastian has drowned?

CAPTAIN:

Madam, after our ship split apart

I saw your brother bind himself

To a strong mast in the sea

Where, like Arion the poet, who rode upon the dolphin's back

He rode upon the waves as far as I could see.

VIOLA:

For saying so, there's gold. Knowst thou this country?

CAPTAIN:

Ay, madam, I was bred and born
Not three hours from this very place.
A noble duke Orsino governs here.

VIOLA:

Orsino! I have heard my father name him. He was a bachelor then.

CAPTAIN:

So he is now, I am sure. I left here a month ago.
People talked then—well, you know,
What great ones do, the people will prattle of.
They said then that their Duke Orsino did seek the love of fair Olivia.

(Viola and the Captain talk quietly as narrator speaks to audience.)

NARRATOR:

Viola is very interested in the story of the lovely Olivia who mourns her brother. She tells the captain she wishes she could work for Lady Olivia as her servant. But the captain tells her that will be difficult as Olivia will see no one. Then she tells the captain she will serve the Duke instead—if he will help her disguise herself as a young boy.

CAPTAIN:

Be you his youth and I'll be mute.
When my tongue blabs, then let mine eyes not see.

VIOLA:

I thank thee. Lead me on.

(EXIT ALL.)

ACT I
Scene 3

Olivia's house.

(ENTER SIR TOBY and SIR ANDREW. They should be joking and punching each other's shoulders and doing little jigs. They may occasionally take a drink from a jug or beer stein, but should not overdo the tipsy behavior.)

NARRATOR:

Behind me you see a couple of comic characters. Lady Olivia's uncle, Sir Toby Belch, and Sir Andrew Aguecheek are pals who are often up to no good. They spend a lot of time drinking and partying. Olivia's servant Maria tries to persuade Sir Toby to calm down and act his age, but you'll find out later that she likes him, and she likes a good joke herself.

(EXIT SIR ANDREW. ENTER MARIA.)

SIR TOBY:

Why does my niece take the death of her brother so hard?

MARIA:

By my troth, Sir Toby, you must come in earlier of nights. Your niece, my lady, takes great exception to your ill hours. You must confine yourself.

SIR TOBY:

Confine? Why, I'm fine enough as I am!

MARIA:

That quaffing and drinking will undo you.

I heard my lady talk of it yesterday and also of a clownish knight that you brought in to woo her.

SIR TOBY:

Sir Andrew Aguecheek? Why, he has three thousand ducats a year!

MARIA:

Ay, but he may have only a year to spend them in, as he's a very clown and a prodigal. And he is drunk nightly in your company.

SIR TOBY:

Here comes Sir Andrew Agueface!

(ENTER SIR ANDREW.)

SIR ANDREW:

Sir Toby Belch! How now, Sir Toby Belch?

SIR TOBY:

Sweet Sir Andrew!

SIR ANDREW:

(To Maria.) Bless you, fair shrew.

MARIA:

And you too, sir.

(They all bow to each other in an exaggerated greeting. Sir Andrew should look silly, bowing with great sweeps of his hand and his toe pointed.)

MARIA:

Fare you well, gentlemen.

SIR ANDREW:

Fair lady, do you think you have fools in hand?

MARIA:

Sir, I do not have you by the hand.

SIR ANDREW:

But you shall have! And here is my hand.
(He takes her hand but she drops it.)

(MARIA EXITS.)

SIR TOBY:

O knight, you need a cup of canary wine!
When did I see thee so put down?

SIR ANDREW:

In faith, I'll be home tomorrow, Sir Toby. Your niece will not be seen; or if she be, it's four to one she'll see none of me. The count himself woos her.

SIR TOBY:

She'll have none of the count. There's life in it yet, man, so do not go home yet.

SIR ANDREW:

I'll stay a month longer! Come! Shall we set about some revels?

SIR TOBY:

What shall we do else?

(Both men grab their mugs from the table, link arms, and do a jig. EXIT.)

ACT I
Scene 4

Duke's palace.

NARRATOR:

Disguised as a young man, Viola has become quite a favorite in the duke's court. Duke Orsino knows her only as his new servant, Cesario. But a surprising twist has developed. Not only does Viola feel very loyal to her new master, the duke, she has also fallen in love with him! Of course he thinks she is a boy, and he has no idea of her secret love for him.

(ENTER VALENTINE and CESARIO, who is Viola dressed as a boy.)

VALENTINE:

If Duke Orsino continues these favors toward you, Cesario, you are likely to be much advanced. He has known you only three days, and already you are no stranger.

CESARIO:

I thank you. Here comes the count.

(ENTER DUKE. CURIO and ATTENDANTS can come onstage with him, but have no lines, so aren't essential).

DUKE ORSINO:

Cesario, I have revealed to you my secret soul.
Therefore, go to Lady Olivia and do not let them send you away.
Tell her my passion, reveal my love!
Surprise her with talk of my dear faith!
She will attend you better because of your youth.

CESARIO:

I think not so, my lord.

DUKE ORSINO:

Dear lad, believe it.

CESARIO:

I'll do my best to woo your lady.
(Aside to the audience.) Oh, but this has difficulties!
Whoever I woo for him, I myself would be his wife.

NARRATOR:

Viola—who is now pretending to be Cesario—wants to do as the duke wishes, but it is so difficult because now she is in love with him herself. Still, she agrees to go to Olivia's house and get past the gates Olivia has ordered kept shut. Olivia says OK, let the young messenger in, but she insists on keeping a veil over her face.

ACT I
Scene 5

Olivia's house.

(ENTER MARIA and FESTE THE CLOWN.)

MARIA:

Either tell me where thou hast been . . . or my lady will hang thee for thy absence.

FESTE:

Let her hang me! He that is hanged in this world needs to fear no enemies.

MARIA:

Peace, you rogue!

(EXIT MARIA.)

(ENTER OLIVIA and her servant MALVOLIO.)

FESTE:

Wit, and it be thy will, has put me into good fooling! Better a witty fool than a foolish wit! God bless thee, lady!

MALVOLIO:

I marvel your ladyship takes delight in such a barren rascal.

OLIVIA:

Oh, Malvolio, you are vain and out of temper. There is no slander in an allowed fool.

(ENTER MARIA.)

MARIA:

Madam, there is at the gate a young gentleman much desires to speak with you. Sir Toby, your kinsman, holds him back.

OLIVIA:

Fetch him off. Sir Toby speaks nothing but madman. Go you, Malvolio. If it be a suit from the count, I am sick or not at home.

(EXIT MARIA and MALVOLIO.)

(MALVOLIO RE-ENTERS.)

MALVOLIO:

Madam, yonder young fellow swears he will speak with you. I told him you were sick; he pretends to know that and therefore comes to speak with you. I told him you were asleep; he seems to know that too and therefore comes to speak with you. What is to be said to him, lady?

OLIVIA:

Tell him he shall not speak with me.

MALVOLIO:

Has been told so, and he says he'll stand at your door like a sheriff's post and be the supporter of a bench. But he WILL speak with you.

OLIVIA:

Of what personage and years is he?

MALVOLIO:

Not yet old enough for a man, nor young enough for a boy.

OLIVIA:

Let him approach. Call in my gentlewoman to throw a veil over my face. Once again, we'll hear Duke Orsino's message.

(MALVOLIO EXITS.)

(MARIA ENTERS with a veil and arranges it over Olivia's face. ENTER VIOLA dressed as Cesario.)

CESARIO:

The honorable lady of the house, which is she?

OLIVIA:

Speak to me.

CESARIO:

Most radiant, exquisite, and unmatchable beauty—I pray you tell me if this be the lady of the house, for I never saw her. I would be loath to cast away my speech. For, besides the fact that it is excellently well penned, I have taken great pains to learn it and it is poetical.

OLIVIA:

I pray you, keep it in. I heard you were saucy at my gates. If you be not mad, be gone; if you have reason, be brief.

CESARIO:

What I am, and what I would, are secret. To your ears, divinity; to any other's profane.

(Olivia nods at Maria, dismissing her. MARIA EXITS.)

CESARIO:

My lord and master loves you.

OLIVIA:

How does he love me?

CESARIO:

With adorations, tears, sighs of fire.

OLIVIA:

I cannot love him.
He is virtuous, noble,
Of great estate, and of fresh and stainless youth . . .
Yet I cannot love him. He might have took his answer long ago.

CESARIO:

If I did love you as he does, I would find no sense in that.

OLIVIA:

Why, what would you do?

CESARIO:

Make me a willow cabin at your gate
Write loyal songs of love and sing them loud even in the dead of night.
Halloa your name to the hills
And make the babbling gossip of the air
Cry out "Olivia!"

OLIVIA:

You might do much. What is your parentage?

CESARIO:

I am a gentleman.

OLIVIA:

Get you to your lord.

I cannot love him. Let him send no more . . .
Unless, perchance, you come to me again
To tell me how he takes it.
Here, spend this for me.

CESARIO:

(Waves away her money.)
Keep your purse. Farewell, fair cruelty.

(CESARIO EXITS.)

OLIVIA:

(Gazing after Viola.)
I swear thou art a gentleman.
Methinks I feel this youth's perfections
Creep in at mine eyes . . . Malvolio!

(ENTER MALVOLIO.)

MALVOLIO:

Here, madam, at your service.

OLIVIA:

Run after that same peevish messenger.
He left this ring behind him.

(Malvolio accepts the ring, bows, and EXITS.)

NARRATOR:

What has Olivia done now? She sends the message that Cesario should return tomorrow so that she can explain why she won't see Duke Orsino. But the real reason Olivia wants to see Cesario again is that she herself has become fond of him!

(OLIVIA EXITS.)

(MUSIC.)

ACT II
Scene 1

Seacoast or beach.

NARRATOR:

On the other side of the island from Olivia and the duke, Viola's brother

Sebastian talks with Antonio, the young man who rescued him from the shipwreck.

(ENTER ANTONIO and SEBASTIAN. Sebastian should be dressed exactly like Cesario and have hair styled the same way.)

NARRATOR:

Sebastian tells Antonio his name and where he comes from and that he has a sister—he HAD a sister, he says, because now he is afraid Viola has drowned. He says that Viola was very intelligent by all accounts, looked very much like him, but was considered beautiful by everyone. Antonio tells Sebastian that he has many enemies here in Duke Orsino's court because he was once engaged in a sea battle with Orsino and was accused of stealing his property. He must be careful not to be seen.

ANTONIO:

Will you stay no longer? May I go with you?

SEBASTIAN:

Be patient with me—but no. My stars shine darkly over me and
my fate might color yours darker. Let me wander.

ANTONIO:

But let me know where you are bound.

SEBASTIAN:

No, sooth, sir. But I can tell you are modest and won't try to pull out me what I prefer to keep in. Therefore, let me express myself.

ANTONIO:

Hold, sir, here's my purse.
Your eye may light upon some toy you desire to purchase.

SEBASTIAN:

I'll be your purse bearer and leave you for an hour. I am bound to Count Orsino's court. Farewell. I will meet you at our lodging.

(SEBASTIAN EXITS.)

ANTONIO:

The gentleness of the gods go with thee!
I have many enemies in Duke Orsino's court, else I would take you there.

(ANTONIO EXITS.)

ACT II
Scene 2

Street.

(ENTER CESARIO. ENTER MALVOLIO, running after her from same side of stage.)

NARRATOR:

When Cesario gets the ring, he will certainly understand the beautiful lady's message. She likes him! Poor Viola! She certainly never could have predicted this would happen, and she certainly doesn't want Olivia to be in love with this person she is pretending to be!

MALVOLIO:

(Haughtily.) The Countess Olivia returns this ring to you, sir. You might have saved me my pains, to have taken it away yourself.

(MALVOLIO EXITS.)

CESARIO:

But I left no ring with her! What means this lady?
Heaven forbid, my outside has charmed her! She loves me sure.
How will all this work out?
O Time, thou must untangle this, not I;
It is too hard a knot for me to untie!

(CESARIO EXITS.)

ACT II
Scene 3

Olivia's house.

(Night. Actor could run across or stand onstage holding Moon up in sky.)

(ENTER ANDREW, SIR TOBY, and FESTE, goofing around, dancing, pretending to trip each other, etc.)

(MUSIC: In original play, Feste sings this song, but could also play recorded song.)

O mistress mine, where are you roaming?
O, stay and hear! Your true love's coming,
That can sing both high and low.
Trip no further, pretty sweeting;
Journeys end in lovers meeting
Every wise man's son doth know.

(ENTER MARIA.)

MARIA:

What a caterwauling do you keep here!

SIR TOBY:

(Sings.) "Three merry men be we!" Am I not consanguineous? Tilly-vally, lady! *(Sings.)* "There dwelt a man in Babylon!" Lady, lady!

MARIA:

Peace! PEACE!

(ENTER MALVOLIO, angrily shaking his fist.)

MALVOLIO:

My masters, are you mad? Or what are you?
Have you no wit, manners, nor honesty, but to gabble like tinkers at this time of night? Is there no respect of place, persons, nor time in you?

SIR TOBY:

Go rub your chain with crumbs! A stoup of wine, Maria!

MALVOLIO:

Mistress Mary, if you prized my lady's favor, you would not allow this uncivil rule. She shall know of it by this hand!

(MALVOLIO EXITS.)

MARIA:

Go shake your ears!

(The other three dance and act silly. Maria shakes her head at them, but she does not appear very angry. She beckons them to come close to her and acts as if she's telling them a secret while the Narrator makes the following speech.)

NARRATOR:

If you're a smart audience and if our actors are doing a good job, you have probably noticed that Sir Toby Belch and Andrew and Maria delight in teasing Malvolio. Maria thinks Malvolio is a conceited tattle-tale. She decides that she wants to play a huge joke on him. She tells the others that she is going to write a letter in her lady's handwriting, swearing undying love for Malvolio, and she thinks Malvolio is just foolish enough and gullible enough to believe the letter is really from Olivia.

MARIA:

I will pretend to praise the color of his beard, the shape of his leg, the expression of his eye, forehead, and complexion. I can write very like my lady your niece.

SIR TOBY:

Excellent! I smell a device.

SIR ANDREW:

I have it in my nose too!

SIR TOBY:

He shall think by the letters you drop that they come from my niece, and that she's in love with him.

SIR ANDREW:

O, 'twill be admirable!

(EXIT ALL.)

ACT II
Scene 4

Duke's palace.

(ENTER DUKE and VIOLA.)

DUKE ORSINO:

Young as you are, you seem as if you have loved. Have you not, boy?

CESARIO:

A little, by your favor.

DUKE ORSINO:

What kind of woman is it?

CESARIO:

Of your complexion.

DUKE ORSINO:

She is not worth thee, then. What years?

CESARIO:

About your years, my lord.

DUKE ORSINO:

Too old, by heaven! Let the woman take
An elder than herself
So their love is more level.

(They sit and talk.)

NARRATOR:

The duke instructs young Cesario on matters of love. He says that men's fancies are "more giddy and unfirm" than women's are. They are "more longing, wavering, sooner lost and won." Cesario tells the duke that somewhere there may be a woman who loves him with the same fierceness that he loves Lady Olivia, but the duke refuses to believe it.

CESARIO:

My father had a daughter loved a man
As I would perhaps love your lordship were I a woman.

DUKE ORSINO:

And what's her history?

CESARIO:

A blank, my lord. She never told her love
But let concealment like a worm in the bud
Feed upon her damask cheek.

DUKE ORSINO:

But died thy sister of her love?

CESARIO:

I am all the daughters of my father's house
And all the brothers too, and yet I know not.
But sir, shall I go now to my lady?

DUKE ORSINO:

Ay, in haste! Give her this jewel.

(EXIT DUKE and CESARIO.)

ACT II
Scene 5

Outside Olivia's house.

NARRATOR:

In the final scene of this act, Maria and her friends Sir Toby and Sir Andrew gather to watch Malvolio make a fool of himself. Poor, vain Malvolio! He finds the letter and he believes that it was written by his mistress, the Lady Olivia. The letter urges him to smile and be happy because she loves him. It urges him to wear yellow, which Maria chose on purpose because it's a color Olivia doesn't like, and to wear criss-crossed garters with his hose—a rather silly fashion of the time.

(ENTER MARIA, SIR TOBY, and SIR ANDREW.)

MARIA:

Get you all three into the box tree! Malvolio's coming down this walk. He has been yonder in the sun practicing behavior to his own shadow for half an hour.

(Maria throws a letter down, and all three scurry behind a tree or screen as Malvolio approaches.)

(ENTER MALVOLIO.)

What have we here? *(Picks up the letter.)* By my life, this is my lady's handwriting! These be her very C's, her U's, and her T's, and this is how she makes her P's. It is certainly her hand. *(He reads.)*
"To the unknown beloved . . ."

SIR ANDREW:

Her C's, her U's, and her T's?

MALVOLIO:

(Reading.) "If this fall into thy hand, revolve. In my stars I am above thee; but be not afraid of greatness. Some are born great, some achieve greatness, and some have greatness thrust upon 'em."
Oh, there is more. See here . . .
(Reading.) "Remember who complimented you on your yellow stockings wished to see thee ever cross-gartered."

(Much laughter from behind the tree.)

MALVOLIO:

(Reading.) "Thou cannot choose but know who I am. If you entertain my love, let it appear in thy smiling."

(Folds up the letter, triumphantly.)

Jove, I thank thee. I WILL smile; I will do everything that you will have me do.

(MALVOLIO EXITS.)

(SIR ANDREW, SIR TOBY, AND MARIA EXIT.)

ACT III
Scene 1

Olivia's garden.

(ENTER CESARIO and OLIVIA.)

CESARIO:

Madam, I come to whet your gentle thoughts on his behalf.

OLIVIA:

O, by your leave, I pray you! I asked you never speak of him;
But, if you were to undertake another suit,
I would rather hear you than any music from the spheres.

CESARIO:

Dear lady—

OLIVIA:

Give me leave, I beseech you.
I did send a ring after you when last you were here.
I fear you must have a hard view of me.
I pray thee, tell me what you think of me.

CESARIO:

That you do think you are not what you are.

OLIVIA:

If I think so, I think the same of you.

CESARIO:

Then think you right, I am NOT what I am.

OLIVIA:

I wish you were as I would have you be!

CESARIO:

And so adieu, good madam. Never more.
Will I my master's tears to you deplore.

OLIVIA:

Yet come again. Maybe you can move
That heart which now abhors to like his love.

(EXIT.)

ACT III
Scene 2

(MARIA ENTERS. MALVOLIO ENTERS, looking ridiculous in yellow stockings with garters criss-crossed up his legs.)

MALVOLIO:

Sweet lady, ho ho!

OLIVIA:

You smile so? I sent for you upon a sad occasion.
What is the matter with thee?

MALVOLIO:

Not black in my mind, though yellow in my legs.
(He sighs and kisses his own hand.)

OLIVIA:

Why do you smile so, and kiss thy hand so often?

MALVOLIO:

"Some are born great"—

OLIVIA:

Huh?

MALVOLIO:

"Some achieve greatness"—

OLIVIA:

What say you?

MALVOLIO:

"And some have greatness thrust upon them."

OLIVIA:

Heaven restore you to your right mind!

MARIA:

Why do you appear with this ridiculous boldness before my lady?

OLIVIA:

Good Maria, call Sir Toby.
Let this fellow be looked to.
This is very midsummer madness.

(EXIT OLIVIA and MARIA.)

MALVOLIO:

O ho! She bids her uncle look after me! Why, everything comes together now! She bids him come so I may appear stubborn to him, for she tells me to in her letter.

(ENTER SIR TOBY and MARIA.)

MALVOLIO:

Go off, I discard you. Let me enjoy my private. Go off!

(EXIT MALVOLIO, trying to look dignified.)

SIR TOBY:

(Laughing.) We will make him mad! Come, Maria, we'll have him in a dark room and bound. My niece already thinks that he is mad.

(ENTER SIR ANDREW. He waves a piece of paper and the others examine it.)

NARRATOR:

The plot thickens. Sir Toby and Maria know that Malvolio is not really crazy. Now they play an even nastier trick on him. They tie him up and leave him in a darkened room. Meanwhile, in a whole new development, Sir Andrew—who still hopes to win Olivia's hand in marriage—has become jealous of the young messenger Cesario who keeps coming to the house. He can tell that Olivia has fallen in love with Cesario and he wants to challenge him to a duel.

SIR ANDREW:

This is the challenge! Read it. It's saucy. I warrant there's vinegar and pepper in it.

SIR TOBY:

(Reading.) "I will waylay you going home and if it be your chance to kill me, you kill me like a rogue and a villain." I'll give him the letter.

(EXIT SIR ANDREW.)

SIR TOBY:

(Tears up the letter.) I'll not deliver the letter. The young gentleman Cesario is of good breeding, and this letter sounds excellently ignorant. He will find it comes from a clodpoll. I will, however, deliver his challenge by word of mouth.

NARRATOR:

Sir Toby's mischievousness knows no limit. Neither Cesario nor Sir Andrew has any will to fight, but Toby's plan is to get them both terrified of each other before they even meet.

(ENTER CESARIO.)

SIR TOBY:

Gentleman, God save thee!

CESARIO:

And you, sir.

SIR TOBY:

Young sir, I do not know what wrongs you have done him, but Sir Andrew awaits you at the orchard, full of anger and bloody as the hunter. Beware. Draw thy sword for he is quick, skillful, and deadly.

CESARIO:

(Terrified.) You mistake me, sir. No man has any quarrel with me!

SIR TOBY:

You'll find it otherwise, I assure you. Be on guard! He is a devil knight. He has separated three souls from their bodies.

CESARIO:

I ask you, please discover what my offense is to him.

SIR TOBY:

I will do so.

CESARIO:

I am no fighter. I will return again to the house.

(EXIT CESARIO.)

NARRATOR:

Sir Toby now tells Sir Andrew that Cesario is just dying for a bloody duel and that he is a fierce warrior. Neither Andrew nor poor Cesario wishes to fight. But just as their duel is about to begin, who should come to Cesario's rescue but Captain Antonio? Oh no! Antonio will think that Cesario is Viola's brother Sebastian. Just keep watching.

(ENTER SIR TOBY and SIR ANDREW, followed by CESARIO.)

SIR TOBY:

There's no remedy, sir. He WILL fight with you.

CESARIO:

Pray God, defend me!

(They start to fight—both terrified. They barely can bring themselves to touch swords.)

(ENTER ANTONIO.)

ANTONIO:

Put up your sword! If this young gentleman have done offense, I take the fault on me.

(Everyone looks astonished.)

(ENTER one or two OFFICERS from Duke Orsino's court. They grab Antonio.)

OFFICER:

I arrest you on the authority of Duke Orsino.

ANTONIO:

You do mistake me, sir.

(Officer grabs him.)

ANTONIO:

(To Cesario.) I must ask you for some of that money.

CESARIO:

What money, sir? I have no money of yours, but I can lend you something.

ANTONIO:

Will you deny me now? After all I have done for you? *(He is being dragged away.)* This youth before you I snatched from the jaws of death.

CESARIO:

But sir, I do not know you by voice or feature!

ANTONIO:

Oh heavens themselves! Sebastian, you have disgraced yourself!

OFFICER:

Come away.

(EXIT ANTONIO and OFFICERS.)

CESARIO:

His words come from such anger . . . he does believe himself. And he did call me Sebastian . . . Oh, prove true, brother, that I were mistaken for you!

(EXIT CESARIO.)

SIR TOBY:

A very dishonest, paltry boy! Leaving his friend here in necessity . . .

SIR ANDREW:

I'll go after him again and beat him!

(EXIT ALL.)

ACT IV
Scene 1

Olivia's house.

NARRATOR:

Approaching Olivia's house, Sebastian has run into Feste the clown. Naturally, when Feste sees someone who looks exactly like Cesario, he assumes that the young man really is Cesario. Olivia has ordered him to bring Cesario back to her, so the clown convinces Sebastian to come with him. Poor Sebastian next meets up with Sir Andrew and Sir Toby and is mistaken for Cesario yet again.

(Feste takes Cesario by the arm and leads him back to Olivia's house.)

(ENTER SIR TOBY and SIR ANDREW.)

(ENTER SEBASTIAN from opposite side of the stage.)

SIR ANDREW:

Now, sir, I meet you again! There's for you! *(Prepares to fight.)*

SEBASTIAN:

Why, there's for you! And there! *(Blow.)* And there! *(Blow.)* Are ALL the people mad here?

(Sir Toby draws his own sword to defend his friend, but doesn't have a chance.)

(ENTER OLIVIA.)

OLIVIA:

Hold, Toby! On my life, I charge thee hold!
You ungracious wretch! Out of my sight!
(To Sebastian.) Be not offended, dear Cesario.
(To Sir Toby.) Be gone!

(EXIT SIR TOBY and SIR ANDREW.)

NARRATOR:

Of course, now Olivia thinks Sebastian is Cesario, the young man she is in love with. What a case of mistaken identity! Sebastian has no idea what's going on, but he sees no harm in going along with it.

(Olivia takes Sebastian by the arm).

OLIVIA:

I pray thee, gentle friend. Go with me to my house,
And hear how many fruitless pranks that ruffian has botched up.
Come, I pray thee. If only you would be ruled by me.

SEBASTIAN:

What is this? If this is a dream, let me sleep!

(EXIT ALL.)

ACT IV
Scene 2

(ENTER MARIA and FESTE the clown.)

(Malvolio is locked up in a dark closet or behind a screen, crouching miserably.)

MARIA:

Put on this parson's gown. Make him believe you are Sir Topas the parson. Hurry!

(She helps Feste into a parson's robe. Feste walks toward Malvolio.)

(ENTER SIR TOBY.)

MALVOLIO:

Who calls there?

FESTE:

Sir Topas the parson, who comes to visit Malvolio the lunatic.

MALVOLIO:

Sir Topas, Sir Topas, good Sir Topas. Go to my lady!

FESTE:

Ah, here is a demon! He can speak of nothing but ladies!

MALVOLIO:

Good sir, I am not mad. They have laid me here in hideous darkness.

FESTE:

Sayst thou that house is dark? But you have high windows.

SIR TOBY:

(In a stage whisper) Now speak to him in your own voice. And come by and by to my chamber. I dare not anger my niece any more.

(EXIT SIR TOBY and MARIA.)

FESTE:

(Singing.) Hey Robin, jolly Robin! Tell me how thy lady does.

MALVOLIO:

Clown! Oh good Clown! Pray, bring me a candle, and pen and ink and paper so that I might write my lady.

FESTE:

(As the parson.) Alas sir, how did you lose your wits?

MALVOLIO:

I am as well in my wits as you, dear Clown.

FESTE:

Then you are mad indeed, if you be no more in your wits than a clown!

MALVOLIO:

Please, some light and some paper.

FESTE:

I will help you to it.

(EXIT FESTE, as himself, singing: "I am gone, sir, and anon, sir, I'll be with you again in a trice!")

(EXIT MALVOLIO.)

ACT IV
Scene 3

The street.

(ENTER SEBASTIAN, examining a jewel in his hand.)

NARRATOR:

Sebastian still wonders if he might be mad. Things are happening very fast. Lady Olivia has just given him a pearl.

SEBASTIAN:

This is the air. That is the glorious sun.
This is the pearl she has just given me. I do feel it and see it.
This is not madness. Where is Antonio?
His counsel would do me golden service now.
Am I mad or is the lady mad? But here she comes!

(ENTER LADY OLIVIA and a PRIEST.)

LADY OLIVIA:

Blame me not for being hasty!
If you mean well truly, come with me and this holy man.
Pledge me your faith,
So that my jealous and doubtful soul
May be at peace!

SEBASTIAN:

I'll follow this good man and you
And having sworn truth, ever will be true.

(EXIT ALL.)

ACT V
Scene 1

Duke's palace.

(ENTER DUKE, CESARIO. From opposite side of stage, ENTER ANTONIO and OFFICER.)

CESARIO:

Here comes the man, sir, that did rescue me!

DUKE ORSINO:

I remember that face well.

Though when I saw it last,

It was smeared black in the face of war.

NARRATOR:

The duke is not happy to see Antonio's face again. He claims Antonio stole his best sea vessel in battle, and he will never forgive him.

CESARIO:

But he did me kindness, sir.

DUKE ORSINO:

Notable pirate! Saltwater thief!

What clownish boldness brings you here?

ANTONIO:

Orsino, noble sir. I never was thief or pirate.

I did rescue that most ungrateful boy there by your side.

I pulled him from the rude sea's enraged and foamy mouth.

DUKE ORSINO:

Fellow, thy words are madness.

For three months this youth has tended upon me.

But more of that later—

(ENTER OLIVIA.)

OLIVIA:

(To the duke.) What would you have, my lord,

Except that which you cannot have? *(Suddenly sees Cesario.)*

Cesario! You do not keep your promise with me.

CESARIO:

Madam!

DUKE ORSINO:

Still so cruel?

OLIVIA:

Still so constant, lord.

NARRATOR:

Poor Duke Orsino. It is almost too much for him now to be confronted with the woman he loves so much, only to find that she is still as indifferent to him as ever.

DUKE ORSINO:

What, so perverse! Come, boy, with me.

OLIVIA:

Where goes Cesario?

CESARIO:

After him I love
More than I love these eyes, more than my life,
More than I shall ever love a wife.

OLIVIA:

Oh, how I am beguiled!
Have you forgot yourself?
Has it been so long since we went with the priest this morning?

DUKE ORSINO:

Come, away!

OLIVIA:

Where, my lord? Whither? Cesario, husband, stay.

DUKE ORSINO:

HUSBAND?

OLIVIA:

Call forth the holy father!

(ENTER PRIEST.)

OLIVIA:

O welcome, Father! Tell what thou know has newly passed
Between this youth and me.

PRIEST:

A contract of eternal bond of love—

DUKE ORSINO:

O thou dissembling cub!

CESARIO:

My lord, I do protest—

(ENTER SIR ANDREW, SIR TOBY, and FESTE. Andrew and Toby are staggering.)

ANDREW:

Send a surgeon! That youth there *(Points to Cesario.)* has broke my head across and given Toby a bloody coxcomb too!

DUKE ORSINO:

My gentleman Cesario?

CESARIO:

(To Andrew.) Why do you speak to me? I never hurt you.
You drew your sword upon me without cause, but I hurt you not.

SIR TOBY:

I hate a drunken rogue. *(Falls over.)*

OLIVIA:

Away with him.

ANDREW:

I'll help you, Sir Toby.

OLIVIA:

Get him to bed and let his hurt be looked to.

(Sir Toby pushes him away.)

(EXIT TOBY, ANDREW, and FESTE.)

(ENTER SEBASTIAN.)

SEBASTIAN:

I am sorry, madam. I have hurt your kinsman, but—

(Olivia gasps at the sight of him. Duke gasps. Antonio gasps. Viola gasps.)

DUKE ORSINO:

One face, one voice, one habit, and two persons!

SEBASTIAN:

Antonio! My dear friend Antonio! How have the hours racked and tortured me since I last saw you!

OLIVIA:

Most wonderful!

ANTONIO:

Have you made division of yourself? An apple cleft in two is not more twin than these two creatures. Which is Sebastian?

SEBASTIAN:

Do I stand there? I never had a brother. I did have a sister
Whom the blind waves and surges have devoured.
Tell me, please—of what country are you? What name?
What parentage?

CESARIO:

Of Messaline. Sebastian was my father—
Sebastian was my brother too, till he went to his watery tomb.

SEBASTIAN:

If you were a woman, I would let my tears fall upon your cheek
And say, "Thrice welcome, drowned Viola!"

CESARIO:

My father had a mole upon his brow—

SEBASTIAN:

So had mine.

CESARIO:

And died the day Viola from her birth numbered thirteen years.

SEBASTIAN:

He did!

CESARIO:

If nothing is in our way but this man's attire,
Which I wore only to serve this noble Duke,
Let me don my maiden clothes.

DUKE ORSINO:

Boy, thou has said a thousand times
Thou should never love woman the way you love me.

CESARIO:

And all those sayings I will swear again.

DUKE ORSINO:

Give me thy hand
And let me see thee in thy woman's weeds.

(MUSIC.)

NARRATOR:

It seems the end of our play must be near, as soon as Viola will put on
her own clothes and appear before the Duke and her brother. But there is

one little problem—the captain who has her clothes is being held in jail for some infraction charged by Malvolio.

OLIVIA:

Malvolio! I now remember.
But they say he is much distracted from his mind.

(ENTER FESTE with a letter in his hand.)

FESTE:

Malvolio has here writ a letter to you.

(Olivia opens the letter and reads it.)

OLIVIA:

Fetch him hither.

(ENTER MALVOLIO.)

DUKE ORSINO:

Is this the madman?

MALVOLIO:

Madam, you have done me wrong!

OLIVIA:

Have I, Malvolio? No.

MALVOLIO:

(Handing her a note.) Study this.
You must not deny it is in your hand.
Did you not bid me to come before you all smiling and cross-gartered,
To put on yellow stockings and to frown upon Sir Toby?
And when I did what you asked, was I not kept in a dark house?
Tell me why.

OLIVIA:

Alas, Malvolio, this is not my writing, though much like it.
Without question it is Maria's hand.

NARRATOR:

When the full extent of that prank has been revealed, it also comes out that Sir Toby has married Maria.

FESTE:

And so the whirligig of time brings in his revenges.

MALVOLIO:

Revenges! I'll be revenged on the whole pack of you!

(EXIT MALVOLIO.)

OLIVIA:

He has been most notoriously abused.

DUKE ORSINO:

Follow him and entreat him to a peace.
When it is known and the time is right
Soon a solemn combination shall be made
Of our dear souls. Meantime, sweet sister,
We will not part from hence.
(Gives Cesario his arm.)

Cesario, come—
For so you shall be while you are a man
But when in other habits you are seen,
Orsino's mistress and his fancy's queen.

(EXIT ALL but Feste the clown. Viola should appear in girl's clothing during curtain call. Feste sings first and last verses. Same music plays during curtain call.)

When that I was and a little tiny boy,
With hey, ho, the wind and the rain,
A clownish thing was but a toy,
For the rain it raineth every day.

A great while ago the world begun,
With hey, ho, the wind and the rain;
But that's all one, our play is done,
And we'll strive to please you every day.

(EXIT FESTE.)

Romeo and Juliet

Juliet. *A gown with simple lines is suitable
for Juliet or any other young female character.
A headpiece and sandals complete this costume.*

It is hard to believe that in our world, Romeo and Juliet would be high school students. In sixteenth-century Italy, girls of noble families were married off at thirteen to men their parents selected. There was no adolescence.

Seeing or reading *Romeo and Juliet* for the first time, children and teenagers are usually impressed by the characters' youth, but they always seem to find the young lovers authentic. This is Shakespeare's genius: Romeo and Juliet are believable for that time and for this time. Shakespeare shows us two recognizable teenagers—not two adults. Against the oppressive reality of their situation, Romeo's and Juliet's youthful eagerness, romanticism, and determination show in stark contrast.

The plot is familiar to most of us, whether we know the play or have seen or read one of the many interpretations of it. Shakespeare himself borrowed the plot from a poem, and he wrote the play in 1594, when his own youth was not far behind him.

Romeo and Juliet are from feuding families in Verona. Romeo loves Juliet the moment he sees her at a masked ball, and he wastes no time in declaring his love. Meanwhile, Juliet's parents want her to marry an older man, Count Paris, and she has agreed to consider him, though she says she has not thought about marriage.

Juliet's temperament is somewhat more measured than Romeo's, though she is just as much in love. She wants to make sure his intent is marriage. When he is banished from the city, she stays behind to plan a way for them to be together. Unfortunately, plans go awry.

Romeo and Juliet is a perfect play for young performers and young audiences. Although it is a tragedy (the title characters kill themselves rather than live without each other), it is not a melodrama, and Romeo and Juliet are not just reckless kids. In fact, there is even something uplifting about this tragedy. Love is such a powerful force, Shakespeare seems to be saying, that when the lovers die for love, their love brings about lasting change. For in a cold vault beside their children's lifeless bodies, Lord Capulet and Lord Montague shake hands and—in the words of the Prince of Verona—make "a glooming peace."

Suggested Music

Canzoni e Danze: Wind Music from Renaissance Italy (compact disc). Piffaro Renaissance Band, Archiv Production, 1995.

Songs & Dances from Shakespeare (compact disc). The Broadside Band, Saydisc Records, 1994.

Come, Gentle Night: Music of Shakespeare's World (compact disc). Ensemble Galilei, Telarc Records, 2000.

Other suggestions for live or recorded music: Renaissance vocal, recorders, guitar.

Suggested Props

Swords

Torch

Basket and herbs (any greenery)

Ring

Vial of sleeping potion

Flowers

Dagger

Suggested Backdrops

Castle

Countryside

Suggested Costumes

Consider using two different colors for members of the Montague and Capulet family, such as red for Montagues and blue for Capulets. This makes it much easier for your audience to identify them.

Romeo, Benvolio, Mercutio: Red, belted doublets (blouses or tunics); black or dark-colored (but not blue) leggings or tight pants; plain hat such as a skull cap, baseball cap worn backward, or yarmulke.

Juliet: Long, blue or white dress; white nightgown or dressing gown (optional).

Nurse: Plain, long, blue dress; white apron if possible; white head covering for wimple, such as a white towel.

Tybalt: Blue, belted doublet (blouse or tunic); black leggings or pants.

Paris: Gold "doublet" (gold silky blouse); cape, if possible (not blue or red); dark leggings or tight pants; boots; hat with feather, if possible.

Prince Escalus of Verona: See suggestions for Paris. Crown instead of hat.

Lords Capulet and Montague: Long robes in the family color (blue or red), such as women's zip-up bathrobe, house coat, or long dress. Coat or cape, if available.

Ladies Capulet and Montague: Long dress, robe, or gown in the family color. Veils, hair up.

Sampson and Gregory: Red, belted doublets (blouses or tunics), dark leggings or tight pants; skull cap or other hat.

Apothecary: Ragged, dirty clothing: torn doublet (blouse or tunic); old leggings or pants. Blouse and leggings in brown or any neutral color—not red or blue.

Friar Laurence: Long, belted monk's robe in brown or black, plain and simple.

Cast of Characters

Chorus/narrator (one or more)
Romeo
Lord Montague, Romeo's father
Lady Montague, Romeo's mother
Benvolio, Montague's nephew and Romeo's friend
Abraham, Montague's servant
Balthazar, Romeo's servant
Juliet
Lord Capulet, Juliet's father
Lady Capulet, Juliet's mother
Tybalt, Juliet's cousin
Juliet's nurse, longtime servant of the Capulets
Peter, Capulet servant
Sampson, Capulet servant
Gregory, Capulet servant
Prince Escalus, Prince of Verona
Mercutio
Count Paris
Friar Laurence
Friar John
Apothecary

Pronunciation Guide to Names

Balthazar (bahl-thuh-zahr)
Benvolio (ben-vol-lee-oh)
Capulet (kap-yoo-let)
Escalus (es-cah-lus)
Mercutio (mer-kyoo-shee-oh)
Montague (mon-tuh-gyoo)
Petruchio (peh-troo-shee-oh)
Tybalt (tih-bult)

Scenes

The street, Capulet house, Montague house, monastery, and Capulet tomb.

Romeo and Juliet

ACT I
Scene 1

(Note: In this play, the Chorus is the narrator and stays onstage at all times. Prologue can be read, printed on program, or left out, at director's discretion.)

Prologue

Two households both alike in dignity
In fair Verona where we lay our scene
From ancient grudge, break to new mutiny,
Where civil blood makes civil hands unclean:
From forth the fatal loins of these two foes,
A pair of star-crossed lovers take their life:
Whose misadventured piteous overthrows,
Doth with their death bury their parents' strife.

Romeo and Juliet

145

The street.

(ENTER CHORUS.)

CHORUS:

Welcome, ladies and gentlemen. Our play takes place in the beautiful city of Verona, Italy, in the sixteenth century. Two noble families have been fighting over a grudge they've been carrying for many years. No one remembers what the fight is really about. Ordinary citizens proclaim their loyalty to one family or the other, and many innocent citizens have been hurt or killed. One of the two families, the Capulets, has a daughter—Juliet—and the other, the Montagues, have a son—Romeo. Romeo is sixteen and Juliet is fourteen, but they are not too young to fall in love. Their love is a sad story, but it is the only thing that eventually causes the two families to stop their feuding.

I am one of the narrators and in this play we are called the Chorus. When we come onstage and stand here, you will know that we will tell you the truth about our tale. In this first scene, you will see two Capulet servants acting silly and then provoking a fight with the Montagues. It will help you keep the two families straight if you remember that Juliet's family, the Capulets, are wearing blue. And Romeo's family, the Montagues, are wearing red.

(SAMPSON and GREGORY ENTER, carrying swords and shields from the house of Capulet).

SAMPSON:

I strike quickly being moved.

GREGORY:

But thou art not quickly moved to strike.

SAMPSON:

A dog of the house of Montague moves me.

GREGORY:

Draw your sword! Here comes one from the house of Montague!

(ENTER BENVOLIO.)

BENVOLIO:

Stop, fools. Put up your swords, you know not what you do.

(Everyone starts to put swords away.)

(ENTER TYBALT. Tybalt looks angry and is hot-tempered and ready to fight.)

TYBALT:

What, art thou drawn among these hartless hinds?
Turn thee, Benvolio, look upon thy death.

BENVOLIO:

I do but keep the peace; put up thy sword.

TYBALT:

What, drawn and talk of peace? I hate the word
As I hate hell, all Montagues, and thee.
Have AT thee, coward!

(Tybalt draws sword. They fight.)

(If there are sufficient cast members for extra citizens, three or more may enter with clubs to join the fight. Various cries follow from the people fighting.)

CITIZEN 1:

Clubs, bills, and partisans!

CITIZEN 2:

Strike them down! Beat them down!

CITIZEN 3:

Down with the Capulets!

CITIZEN 4:

Down with the Montagues!

ACT I
Scene 2

Street, Capulet house.

CHORUS:

At this point everyone in the street appears to be fighting—either in support of the Capulet family or the Montague family. Lord and Lady Capulet, Juliet's parents, get involved. Then Romeo's parents, old Montague and his lady, come in.

(ENTER LORD CAPULET and LADY CAPULET.)

LORD CAPULET:

What noise is this? Give me my long sword, ho!

LADY CAPULET:

A crutch, a crutch; you are an old man, why call you for a sword?

LORD CAPULET:

My sword, I say! Old Montague is come.
And flourishes his blade in spite of me.

(ENTER LORD MONTAGUE and LADY MONTAGUE. Lord Capulet grabs him.)

LORD MONTAGUE:

Thou villain Capulet; hold me not, let me go.

LADY MONTAGUE:

Thou shalt not stir one foot to see a foe.

CHORUS:

Into this fray comes Prince Escalus, the Prince of Verona. He pleads with both sides to stop the fighting and threatens them with losing their lives. Then old Montague appeals to Benvolio, his nephew and a good friend of Romeo's.

(The PRINCE ENTERS.)

PRINCE:

Rebellious subjects, enemies to peace!
Hear the sentence of your Prince.
If ever you disturb our streets again
Your lives shall pay the forfeit of the peace.

(EVERYONE EXITS except Benvolio.)

(ROMEO ENTERS, appearing dejected and sad.)

BENVOLIO:

Romeo, good morrow, cousin.

ROMEO:

Is the day so young? Ay me! Sad hours seem long.

BENVOLIO:

What sadness lengthens Romeo's hours?

ROMEO:

Not having that love which having makes them short.

(Benvolio takes Romeo's arm and talks to him quietly.)

CHORUS:

Benvolio is a good and gentle friend. He tries to cheer Romeo up by telling him that there will be a big party tonight at the Capulets. Of course, since the party is at their enemy's house, they will have to go wearing masks.

(LORD CAPULET, PETER, the servant, and PARIS ENTER. They should occupy opposite end of stage from Benvolio and Romeo.)

CHORUS:

Meanwhile, at his house, Capulet is approached by the nobleman Paris, who wants to marry Juliet. Capulet has already told Paris that Juliet is only fourteen and that he wants Paris to wait two more years before he will consent to the match. But now it seems that Capulet might be changing his mind.

PARIS:

Now, my lord, what say you to my suit?

LORD CAPULET:

Saying over what I said before;
My child is yet a stranger in the world,
She has not seen the change of fourteen years.

PARIS:

Younger than she are happy mothers made.

CHORUS:

Capulet says that Paris may woo Juliet and that if she is in agreement, they have his consent to marry. He invites Paris to come to his house tonight for the big party and sends Peter off with an invitation for the party to everyone on his list.

(ROMEO and BENVOLIO EXIT from their side of stage. CAPULET and PARIS EXIT. Peter squints at the paper, turns it upside down in a some-what clownish fashion because he can't read it. PETER EXITS, waving the paper.)

ACT I
Scene 3

Capulet house.

(LADY CAPULET and NURSE ENTER.)

LADY CAPULET:

Nurse, where's my daughter? Call her forth to me.

NURSE:

What, lamb? What, ladybird? Where's this girl? What, Juliet?

(ENTER JULIET, running.)

JULIET:

How now? Who calls?

NURSE:

Your mother.

JULIET:

Madam, I am here. What is your will?

LADY CAPULET:

Tell me, daughter Juliet, how stands your disposition to be married?

JULIET:

It is an honor that I dream not of.

NURSE:

An honor?

LADY CAPULET:

Well, think of marriage now.

Speak briefly, can you like of Paris's love?

JULIET:

I'll look to like. If looking makes me like him, then I shall.

(EXIT NURSE, JULIET, and LADY CAPULET.)

Act I
Scene 4

The street.

(ENTER ROMEO, MERCUTIO, and BENVOLIO. Mercutio and Benvolio appear ready for a party—jostling each other and having fun, but Romeo is still dejected.)

CHORUS:

Romeo and his friends are outside the Capulets' house, getting ready to go in to the party.

ROMEO:

Let me carry the torch. I will bear the light.

MERCUTIO:

No, gentle Romeo, we must have you dance!

ROMEO:

You have dancing shoes with nimble soles.

I have a soul of lead. But 'tis no wit to go.

BENVOLIO:

Come! Supper is done and we shall come too late.

ROMEO:

Let's go, gentlemen.

(MUSIC leading into party.)

Act I
Scene 5

Capulet house.

(ENTER CAPULET, LADY CAPULET, JULIET, TYBALT, NURSE, and all the GUESTS. MUSIC plays and dancing begins. Lord and Lady Capulet are talking and joking with each other, when ROMEO, BENVOLIO, and MERCUTIO ENTER. Romeo catches sight of Juliet.)

ROMEO:

What lady is that which does enrich the hand of yonder knight?

BENVOLIO:

I know not.

ROMEO:

O she does teach the torches to burn bright!
It seems she hangs upon the cheek of night
As a rich jewel in an Ethiop's ear—
Beauty too rich for use, for earth too dear.

TYBALT:

By the sound of his voice, he is a Montague.
Get me my sword. What, dares he
Come hither, covered with a mask to mock and scorn our festivities!
By my family's honor I wouldn't call it a sin to strike him dead!

LORD CAPULET:

Young Romeo, is it?

TYBALT:

'Tis he, that villain, Romeo!

LORD CAPULET:

Content thee, gentle cuz. Let him alone.
He bears himself like a gentleman.

TYBALT:

When such a villain is a guest
I'll not endure him.
Why uncle, 'tis a shame!

(Capulet is admiring the dancers and complementing them, bowing his head and smiling. Then he turns to Tybalt, sternly.)

LORD CAPULET:

You are a saucy boy. Is it so indeed?

For shame, I'll make you quiet.

TYBALT:

I will withdraw; but this intrusion shall

Now seeming sweet, convert to bitterest gall.

(EXIT TYBALT. Romeo and Juliet move closer to each other.)

ROMEO:

If I profane with my unworthiest hand

This holy shrine, the gentle sin is this:

My lips, two blushing pilgrims, ready stand

To smooth that rough touch with a tender kiss.

JULIET:

Good pilgrim, you do wrong your hand too much.

(MUSIC. They begin to dance slowly, or walk in slow circles, keeping their eyes on each other.)

NURSE:

Madam, your mother craves a word with you.

(Juliet walks away.)

ROMEO:

Who is her mother?

NURSE:

The lady of the house.

ROMEO:

A Capulet! Now I have given my heart to mine enemy!

(The party is winding down. Capulet bids them good night. Romeo is stunned. ALL EXIT except Juliet and Nurse.)

JULIET:

Come hither, nurse. Who is that gentleman?

NURSE:

His name is Romeo and he is a Montague,

The only son of your great enemy!

JULIET:

My only love, sprung from my only hate!

(Lady Capulet's voice calls from offstage: "Juliet!")

NURSE:

Come, let's away; the strangers all are gone.

ACT II
Scene 1

Street beneath Juliet's window.

CHORUS:

Romeo is in love with Juliet and he is loved by her in return. But what can they do? He isn't free to see her, because she is supposed to be his enemy. Still, they are anxious to steal some time to be together. In this scene, it's late at night after the party, and Juliet has gone out to the balcony outside her room. By the time her Nurse starts demanding that she come inside and go to bed, she has already had a sweet conversation with Romeo, who lingers below.

(JULIET ENTERS her "balcony." ROMEO ENTERS, stays below, catches sight of her. She doesn't see him yet.)

ROMEO:

What light through yonder window breaks?
It is the East and Juliet is the sun.

JULIET:

O Romeo, Romeo, wherefore art thou Romeo?
Deny thy father and refuse thy name.
And I'll no longer be a Capulet.
What's in a name? That which we call a rose
By any other word would smell as sweet.

ROMEO:

I take thee at thy word.
Call me but love, and I'll be newly baptized.
Henceforth I never will be Romeo.

JULIET:

My ears have not yet drunk a hundred words
Of thy tongue's uttering, yet I know the sound.
Art thou not Romeo, and a Montague?

ROMEO:

Neither, fair maid, if either you dislike.

JULIET:

If my kinsmen see you, they will murder you.

ROMEO:

Look thou but sweet,
And I am proof against their hatred.

(The two young lovers speak—audience doesn't have to hear them. They are "murmuring sweet nothings" to each other.)

NURSE:

Juliet—

JULIET:

I must go, But if your intentions be honest
And your purpose is marriage
Then give word to one I will send to you tomorrow.

NURSE:

Juliet!

JULIET:

O good night, good night.
Parting is such sweet sorrow that I shall say good night
Till it be morrow.

(EXIT.)

Act II
Scene 2

Outside the monastery.

(ENTER FRIAR LAURENCE with a basket, picking herbs.)

CHORUS:

It is a new day. Romeo's good friend and adviser Friar Laurence is picking herbs in the field around the monastery. Romeo has confided in him many times and trusts his judgment. Now when Romeo goes to him requesting advice about his love for Juliet, the good old priest can hardly believe that Romeo has already forgotten the old love.

(ROMEO ENTERS.)

FRIAR LAURENCE:

Romeo! Why are you up so early?
Or have you not yet been to bed this night?

ROMEO:

It's true! I have been feasting with my enemy,
Where I met one whom I love more than all of the Earth.
Will you marry us?

FRIAR LAURENCE:

I will help you in this cause for one reason:
By this marriage we may put an end to the war between your houses.

Romeo and Juliet

(FRIAR LAURENCE EXITS.)

(MERCUTIO and BENVOLIO ENTER, cross the stage as if looking for something, then EXIT.)

CHORUS:

Meanwhile, Mercutio and Benvolio have been roaming the city all night, looking for their friend. They realize that he never went home after the party. They are looking for him because they have a letter sent to him by Tybalt—Tybalt wants to issue Romeo a challenge for a fight.

ACT II
Scene 3

Monastery.

(MUSIC. ENTER FRIAR LAURENCE, JULIET, and ROMEO.)

(Marriage scene in pantomime: Juliet and Romeo kneel before the friar and bow their head as he performs a silent ceremony. Then they rise and clasp hands or embrace.)

(EXIT ALL.)

ACT III
Scene 1

The street.

CHORUS:

Romeo travels home through the afternoon heat, having vowed to return to Juliet secretly that night. Unfortunately, Juliet's cousin, the fiery Tybalt, has been roving through town. When he encounters Romeo's friends Mercutio and Benvolio, it looks like Tybalt will finally find the fight he has been looking for.

(ENTER MERCUTIO and BENVOLIO.)

BENVOLIO:

I pray thee, good Mercutio, let's retire.
The day is hot, the Capulets are abroad.

MERCUTIO:

Come come, you are as hot-blooded a fellow as any in Italy.

(ENTER TYBALT from the other side of the stage. Tybalt draws his sword. Mercutio and Benvolio look like they would prefer not to fight with him.)

(ENTER ROMEO.)

TYBALT:

(Turning toward Romeo.)
Well, peace be with you, sir, here comes my man!
Romeo, the love I bear you means nothing more than this:
You are a villain.

ROMEO

Tybalt, villain am I none. I see you know me not.

TYBALT:

Boy, this shall not excuse the injuries you have done me.
Therefore, turn and draw!

MERCUTIO:

Tybalt, you rat-catcher, will you walk this way?

(Fight begins. Romeo gets in the way and Tybalt thrusts his sword under Romeo's arm and into Mercutio.)

(Tybalt looks scared.)

MERCUTIO:

(Staggering, dying.)

Ay, ay, a scratch, a scratch. Go, fetch a surgeon.

ROMEO:

Courage, man, the hurt cannot be much.

MERCUTIO:

Why came you between us? I was hurt under your arm!

ROMEO:

I thought all for the best.

MERCUTIO:

 Help me into some house, Benvolio,
Or I shall faint. A plague on both your houses!

BENVOLIO:

O Romeo, Romeo, brave Mercutio is dead.

ROMEO:

Now, Tybalt, take back the "villain" that you called me.
Mercutio's soul is but a little way above our heads.
Either thou or I must go with him.

(They fight and Romeo kills Tybalt.)

(EXIT ALL.)

ACT III
Scene 2

Juliet's chamber.

(JULIET ENTERS. NURSE ENTERS, wringing her hands.)

JULIET:

Now Nurse, what news?

NURSE:

He's killed! He's dead!

JULIET:

Romeo dead?

NURSE:

O courteous Tybalt, honest gentleman!
That ever I should live to see thee dead!

JULIET:

Is Romeo slaughtered AND Tybalt dead?
My dearest cousin and my dearer lord?

NURSE:

No, my lady. Tybalt is dead and Romeo banished.
Romeo that killed him, he is banished.

JULIET:

O serpent heart! O angel-faced fiend!
Romeo, how opposite you are to what you seem!

NURSE:

There's no trust, no faith, no honesty in men.
Shame come to Romeo.

JULIET:

(As if remembering that she loves him.)
O Nurse—find him,
Give this ring to my true knight.
And bid him come to take his last farewell.

(EXIT JULIET and NURSE.)

Act III
Scene 3

Monastery.

(ENTER FRIAR LAURENCE and ROMEO.)

CHORUS:

Romeo has taken refuge with Friar Laurence, but this cannot last long. After all, he has been banished by the prince. The good old Friar is somewhat impatient with Romeo by now. After all, Romeo has committed murder and yet he is complaining bitterly about his punishment. Romeo is very upset.

ROMEO:

Banished? "Banished" is banished from the world!

FRIAR LAURENCE:

The law calls for death but the kind prince has pushed aside the law. This is dear mercy.

ROMEO:

'Tis torture and not mercy. Heaven is here where Juliet lives.

(NURSE ENTERS.)

NURSE:

Here, sir, is a ring she bid me give you, sir.
Go, make haste, for it grows very late.

FRIAR LAURENCE:

Go to Mantua before the break of day, and I'll send news from time to time.

(EXIT ALL.)

Act III
Scene 4

Capulet house.

(On one side of the stage is a pantomime of Romeo and Juliet saying good-bye to each other. They embrace one last time and then EXIT.)

(ENTER LORD CAPULET, LADY CAPULET, and PARIS. They sit and talk.)

CHORUS:

Of course no one besides the Nurse and Friar Laurence know of Romeo and Juliet's secret marriage. Juliet's parents, meanwhile, are still planning her marriage to Paris. Paris is aware that Juliet is grieving for her cousin Tybalt and thinks this is not a good time to court her.

PARIS:

These times of woe afford no times to woo. Madam, good night.
Commend me to your daughter.

LADY CAPULET:

I'll know her mind by early tomorrow.
Tonight she is shut up with her sorrow.

LORD CAPULET:

What day is this?

PARIS:

Monday, my lord.

LORD CAPULET:

Monday! Ah . . . well, Wednesday is too soon.
 A Thursday let it be.
She shall be married to this noble earl on Thursday.

PARIS:

My lord, I would that Thursday were tomorrow.

(ALL EXIT.)

ACT III
Scene 5

Capulet house.

(ENTER JULIET and LADY CAPULET.)

LADY CAPULET:

Ho, daughter, are you up? Why how now, Juliet?

JULIET:

Madam, I am not well.

LADY CAPULET:

Evermore weeping for your cousin's death?
But now I'll tell thee joyful tidings, girl.

JULIET:

Joy comes well in such a needy time.

LADY CAPULET:

Early next Thursday morn
The gallant, young, and noble gentleman, the Count Paris,
At St. Peter's Church, shall happily make thee a joyful bride!

JULIET:

Now by St. Peter's Church and Peter too—
He shall NOT make me there a joyful bride.

LADY CAPULET:

> *(Angrily.)*
> What say you? Here comes your father. Tell him so yourself.

> *(ENTER CAPULET and NURSE. Juliet throws herself at her father's feet.)*

LORD CAPULET:

> How now, what, still in tears?
> Wife, have you delivered to her our decree?

LADY CAPULET:

> Ay sir, but she will none.

JULIET:

> Good father, I beseech you on my knees.
> Hear me with patience but to speak a word—

LORD CAPULET:

> *(Very angrily.)* Disobedient wretch!
> I tell thee what—get thee to church on Thursday
> Or never after look me in the face.

CHORUS:

> Juliet's sadness is very deep and Lord Capulet's anger is very strong. He thinks that he is justified in commanding his only daughter to marry. In his world that is what a noble father is supposed to do—find a good and wealthy gentleman for his daughter's husband. He is used to being obeyed, and he takes Juliet's refusal very hard. And poor Juliet is about to receive yet another betrayal—from her most loyal friend.

> *(EXIT LORD and LADY CAPULET.)*

JULIET:

> Nurse, how shall this be prevented?

NURSE:

> Romeo is banished.
> Likely he will never dare come back to claim you.
> The Count is a lovely gentleman.
> I think you will be happy in this second match.

JULIET:

> Do you speak from the heart?

NURSE:

And from my soul too.

JULIET:

Then tell my mother I am gone.
To Friar Laurence's cell, to make confession
And to be forgiven for displeasing my father.

NURSE:

This is wisely done.

(NURSE EXITS.)

JULIET:

O most wicked fiend.
I will go to the Friar to know what he thinks.
If all else fails, I will take my life!

(JULIET EXITS.)

Act IV
Scene 1

*(ENTER FRIAR LAURENCE from one side of stage.
ENTER JULIET from other side.)*

JULIET:

Come weep with me—past hope, past cure, past help!

FRIAR LAURENCE:

O Juliet, I already know thy grief!
I hear thou must on Thursday next be married to this Count.
I do spy a kind of hope. If you dare, I'll give you a remedy.

*(Friar puts his arm around her shoulders and turns away as if telling
her a secret.)*

CHORUS:

The friar tells Juliet that he has a plan. If she is bold enough to imagine
taking her own life, then he thinks she can go through with his scheme. He
says she should go home, act cheerful, and give her consent to marrying
Count Paris. The next night she should drink the liquid in the vial he gives
her. It will make her go into a deep, deep sleep—in fact, she will appear dead.
But she will not actually be dead. When her nurse and her mother come to

wake her for her wedding day, they will think she is no more. Everyone will mourn her and they will put her in the large, stone family tomb. He will send a message to Romeo. By the time Juliet wakes up from her strange sleep, Romeo will be there to take her to Mantua. Meanwhile, the friar tells Juliet that he will work continuously with the two families to repair the rift between them forever.

JULIET:

Love give me strength.
Farewell, dear father.

(EXIT FRIAR LAURENCE and JULIET.)

ACT IV
Scene 2

Capulet house.

CHORUS:

Wedding preparations are in full swing for the next day in the Capulet household. Lord Capulet is excited and has ordered all the best preparations. Meanwhile, in her chamber, Juliet bids good night to her nurse and to her mother. She prepares to enter her long deathlike sleep. She has the vial of sleeping potion the friar has given her and is trying to summon her courage to take it.

(ENTER JULIET, LADY CAPULET, and NURSE.)

JULIET:

Gentle Nurse, I pray thee leave me to myself tonight.

LADY CAPULET:

Good night. Get thee to bed and rest.

(EXIT LADY CAPULET and NURSE.)

JULIET:

(Holding up the vial of sleeping potion with both hands.)
What if it is a poison the friar has cleverly given me
So he won't be dishonored for performing our marriage?
And yet I think not, for he has always been a holy man.
But what if I wake too soon?
Locked in our family tomb with corpses long dead?

(She shudders and takes the potion.)
Romeo, I come! This do I drink for thee!

(Juliet falls back upon her bed.)

ACT IV
Scene 3

(NURSE ENTERS, holding flowers. She sees Juliet.)

NURSE:

Mistress! What, mistress? Why, lamb, why, lady!
Mistress, sweetheart, you slugabed? How sound is she asleep!
(Nurse looks carefully at Juliet. Touches her.)
Alas, alas! Help help! My lady's dead!

(ENTER LADY CAPULET.)

LADY CAPULET:

What noise is here? O me, O me!
My child, my only life. Revive, look up
Or I will die with thee. Help, help!

(ENTER LORD CAPULET.)

LORD CAPULET:

What? Let me see her! Out, alas. She's cold.
Her blood is settled and her joints are stiff.

NURSE:

O lamentable day!

LADY CAPULET:

O woeful time!

LORD CAPULET:

Death has taken her and makes me wail in grief
Ties my tongue and will not let me speak.

(COUNT PARIS ENTERS; he has heard the news.)

PARIS:

O, have I longed to see this my wedding day.
And does it give me such a sight as this!

LORD CAPULET:

All the things we ordered shall turn this festival day
To a black funeral.
Our instruments turn to melancholy bells
And our bridal flowers serve for a buried corpse.

(ALL EXIT except for Nurse, who lays flowers upon Juliet. EXITS.)

ACT V
Scene 1

The street in Mantua.

CHORUS:

Romeo is in Mantua. He spends his time in the streets, hoping for news delivered by his servant Balthazar, from the friar in Verona.

(ROMEO ENTERS from one side of stage slowly. BALTHAZAR ENTERS from other side and encounters him. They "talk." BALTHAZAR EXITS.)

When Balthazar finally comes, however, it is not with the news poor Romeo has been waiting for. Balthazar does not come to summon him to Juliet's side. In fact, Balthazar comes to tell Romeo that it appears Juliet has died. Romeo has not learned of the friar's plan to fake Juliet's death, so he really thinks she has died. Once he believes she is dead, he wants only to join her in death.

He recalls an old apothecary, a man who sells drugs and potions. Romeo thinks this old man will sell him the deadly poison he needs to kill himself.

(EXIT ROMEO.)

ACT V
Scene 2

CHORUS:

The tragedy is building quickly now. Poor Romeo, who thinks Juliet is dead! Poor Lord and Lady Capulet, who think their daughter is dead! And poor Juliet, who is about to wake up in a cold, dark burial vault all alone. Meanwhile, Friar Laurence has learned an awful truth. The priest he sent to Mantua with news of his plan never reached Romeo. He was kept from even leaving Verona because city officials suspected he'd been visiting a household that was contaminated by the plague.

(ENTER FRIAR LAURENCE and FRIAR JOHN.)

FRIAR LAURENCE:

But who bore my letter to Romeo, then?

FRIAR JOHN:

I could not send it. Here it is again.

FRIAR LAURENCE:

Unhappy fortune! Not having that news could cause much harm.

Friar John, go and get me an iron crowbar and bring it straight to

my cell.

FRIAR JOHN:

Brother, I'll go and bring it to you.

(EXIT FRIAR JOHN.)

FRIAR LAURENCE:

Now must I go to the monument alone.

Within three hours Juliet will wake.

I will send word again to Mantua for Romeo to come and meet her,

But meanwhile I will keep her with me until Romeo comes.

(EXITS.)

ACT V
Scene 3

(Capulet vault. COUNT PARIS ENTERS with flowers. When he hears noise, he hides himself.)

(ROMEO ENTERS the vault, and he and Paris see each other.)

PARIS:

Here is that banished, haughty Montague

Who murdered my love's cousin! We think her grief

Caused the fair creature's death.

Obey and go with me, for thou must die.

ROMEO:

I must indeed.

Please, good and gentle youth. Do not urge me to fury.

Stay not, be gone. Live, and from here on say

A madman's mercy made you run away.

PARIS:

I do defy you and apprehend you for a felon!

ROMEO:

Will you provoke me? Then have at it, boy!

(They fight and Romeo slays Paris.)

PARIS:

O, I am slain!

If you are merciful, open the tomb and lay me with Juliet! *(He dies.)*

CHORUS:

Romeo lays Paris down near Juliet. Then he leans over Juliet and tells her not to fear death, for he will stay with her now forever in this palace of dim night. Meanwhile, he prepares to drink his poison and take his last breath.

ROMEO:

Eyes, look your last. Arms, take your last embrace!

Here's to my love! *(He drinks.)* O true apothecary!

Thy drugs are quick. Thus with a kiss I die. *(He falls.)*

(ENTER FRIAR LAURENCE.)

FRIAR LAURENCE:

Romeo!

(Juliet stirs, stretches, rises.)

JULIET:

O comfortable Friar, where is my lord?

I do remember well where I should be. Where is my Romeo?

FRIAR LAURENCE:

Lady, come away from this nest

Of death and unnatural sleep.

Your husband lies dead and Paris too.

Come, good Juliet. I dare no longer stay.

JULIET:

(Weeping.) Go, get thee hence, for I will not away.

(EXIT FRIAR LAURENCE.)

What's here? A cup closed in my true love's hand?

Poison, I see, has been his timeless end.

What, drunk all, and left no friendly drop
To help me follow after? I will kiss thee.
Maybe some poison does remain—
Oh, thy lips are warm!

(She hears noises of people approaching.)
I'll be brief. O happy dagger!
(She takes Romeo's dagger from his belt).
There, rust, and let me die.
(She stabs herself and falls.)

*(Gradually the stage fills up with people: BALTHAZAR, PRINCE
ESCALUS, CAPULET and LADY CAPULET, MONTAGUE, and
FRIAR LAURENCE.)*

PRINCE:

What misadventure is so early up that calls us from our morning rest?

LORD CAPULET:

What should it be that is so shrieked abroad?

LADY CAPULET:

O, the people in the street cry "Romeo"
And some cry "Juliet" and some "Paris"
And all run toward our monument!

LORD CAPULET:

O heavens! O wife, look how our daughter bleeds!

LORD MONTAGUE:

My wife is dead tonight!
Grief of my son's exile has stopped her breath.
What further woe conspires against mine age?

PRINCE:

Look and thou shall see.

(Lord Montague sees Romeo on the ground.)

LORD MONTAGUE:

O thou untaught boy!
What manners are in this
To press before thy father to a grave!
(He falls over Romeo's body and weeps.)

(Friar Laurence comes forward and bows low before the prince. The prince makes him rise.)

CHORUS:

The friar comes forward and explains everything. He feels that much of what has happened is his fault. The prince tells everyone that these sad events are the result of a scourge of hatred. They are not any one person's fault, but he, too, is partly to blame for having ignored the fighting of the two families for so long. Now it is time to make peace and to learn a lesson from the tragic love of Romeo and Juliet.

PRINCE:

A glooming peace this morning with it brings.
The sun for sorrow will not show his head.
Go hence to talk more of these sad things.
Some will be pardoned and some punished.
For never was a story of more woe
Than this of Juliet and her Romeo.

(EXIT ALL.)

Romeo and Juliet

169

The Tempest

Ariel running in the waves. *Consider an outdoor production if weather permits it. Staging* The Tempest *or any of Shakespeare's plays in the open air evokes the proximity and the drama of nature.*

The *Tempest* begins with the noises of a wild storm and a shipwreck, and it ends with gentle winds and order restored. The ship that founders on the shore of a small island carries with it a royal party from Italy, whose members then get separated but who eventually meet the inhabitants of the island: Prospero, an old sorcerer with unpredictable ways, and his beautiful daughter, Miranda. Strange things happen when these people meet each other—and we learn that some of them have met before.

This is a play full of magic and fantasy, and it belongs to the romance category of Shakespeare's plays. Believed to be Shakespeare's last play, written in 1611 (though he probably collaborated on later scripts), *The Tempest* explores the difference between reality and illusion. It offers up a solid plot, but also gives us magic and characters that disappear. Prospero is a very real man, but when he puts on his magic cloak and takes up his magic staff, he is part of another world that is real only to some. The lively spirit Ariel obediently does Prospero's bidding until the end of the play, when Prospero puts aside his own magic powers and sets Ariel free. Is Ariel real, or does he dwell within his master's imagination?

Children who have studied the explorers will be interested to know that Shakespeare probably based the plot of *The Tempest* on the true account of an English shipwreck. The ship had set sail for the Virginia Colony in 1609, along with eight other ships, but became lost at sea less than two months later in a violent storm. This story of the ship and its inhabitants caught the public imagination when it disappeared and was discovered months later washed up on the shores of Bermuda. Crew and passengers were all alive and well and constructing a new ship.

Shakespeare set his play on a desert island. King Alonso of Naples and his brother Antonio, the Duke of Milan, were sailing back to Italy from North Africa after the wedding of the king's daughter to the prince of Tunis. Ferdinand, the king's son, believes he is the ship's only survivor and is plunged into despair, but his sadness is tempered when he meets Miranda and falls in love immediately. Miranda is equally impressed with him.

When the storm hits, it is sudden and catastrophic—but only for the travelers. For Prospero and for Ariel, it is planned. Using his magic, Prospero has engineered this wreck as a way of bringing to justice those who have sinned against him. The result benefits the innocent and the evildoers alike.

Creating an opportunity for forgiveness is Prospero's last great use of magic. By the end of the play, he is ready to rely on human power alone. In a beautifully moving last speech, Prospero stands alone on the stage and begs the audience for its indulgence:

Now my charms are all o'erthrown,
And what strength I have's mine own, . . .

Many interpret this last play of Shakespeare's as his way of saying good-bye to writing. Like Prospero laying down his staff and removing his magic cloak, Shakespeare puts aside his pen—the instrument that has allowed him to create realities other than his own, to offer up tales of great beauty and mystery.

Suggested Music

Although virtually all Shakespeare's plays include music, few records exist telling us precisely what songs, ballads, or instrumental pieces were indicated in the original productions. *The Tempest* is an exception. Scholars are quite sure that two songs Ariel sings were composed and written for the first production of *The Tempest* in 1611. The first is "Full Fathom Five" in Act I, Scene 2, and the second is "Where the Bee Sucks, There Suck I" in Act V, Scene 1. The words to these songs are included in my script, as they appear in the original text.

To hear these songs as they may have sounded in Shakespeare's time, listen to *Songs & Dances from Shakespeare*, tracks 1 and 2 (The Broadside Band, Saydisc Records, 1994). Other suggestions for recorded music: *Come, Gentle Night: Music of Shakespeare's World* (Ensemble Galilei, Telarc Records, 2000).

The character Ariel (invisible to all but Prospero) is always associated with music. You might want to associate one particular song or sound with Ariel's entrances. As with all the plays, feel free to use any music—child musicians playing any instruments or recorded music of any type.

Suggested Props

Model ship

Prospero's symbols of his magic: staff and mantle/cloak

Musical instrument for Ariel

Swords

Firewood

Bottle

Dried flowers

Crown for Juno

Fruit

Chessboard and pieces

Suggested Backdrops

The sea
A rocky beach

Suggested Costumes

The king and his royal shipmates should conform to your image of Italian noblemen: tunics (long, belted blouses or shirts) and pants are fine, but if you have jackets, capes, hats, boots, and above all, swords—these would all be great.

Prospero's costume can be a simple shirt and pants but should also include a special mantle (cloak or cape) and a rod or staff. These items are important, as they symbolize his magic powers, and are taken off or put on at various points in the play. In the last act, Ariel brings Prospero his ducal robes so that the others recognize who he really is.

Ariel can be played by a boy or a girl. He or she can be a bird with wings or any ethereal-looking creature that conforms to the children's image of a sprite or fairy. The actor can wear tights and a cape, home-made wings, even a collection of scarves tied to a belt. In Act III, Scene 3, Ariel portrays a harpy, a mythical creature with the face of a woman and the wings and talons of a bird. The other spirits in Act IV, Scene 1, should also be dressed imaginatively: Study the scene to get ideas for Iris, Ceres, Juno, and the wild-animal spirits.

Caliban is part human and part monster and can also be played by a child of either gender. The character's wildness and creepiness can be represented in its costume, a scary mask, or creepy makeup. He should have a cape, blanket, or extra-large shirt so he can hide under it in Act II, Scene 2.

Miranda is the only human female: a girl of fifteen. She should wear a plain dress, preferably long, and if the child playing her has long hair, it should be worn down.

Trinculo and Stephano should have pants and shirts that are dirty and/or ripped.

Cast of Characters

Narrator(s)

The ship
Alonso, King of Naples
Sebastian, his brother
Antonio, his brother, the usurping Duke of Milan
Ferdinand, son of the King of Naples
Gonzalo, an honest old counselor

Adrian, nobleman
Francisco, nobleman
Trinculo, servant
Stephano, drunken butler
Master of a ship
Boatswain
Mariners

The island
Prospero, the rightful Duke of Milan
Miranda, daughter of Prospero
Ariel, an airy spirit commanded by Prospero (male or female)
Caliban, a savage and deformed slave
Iris
Ceres
Juno
Nymphs
Other spirits attending Prospero

Casting note: Many characters—Ariel, Caliban, Trinculo, various spirits—can be played by male or female actors. The part of Prospero is comparatively large. Consider casting two children in this role, switching partway through.

Pronunciation Guide to Names

Alonso (uh-lon-zo)
Ariel (air-ee-uhl)
Caliban (kal-uh-ban)
Ceres (seer-eez)
Francisco (fran-sis-ko)
Gonzalo (gon-zah-loh)
Juno (joo-noh)
Prospero (pros-per-oh)
Sebastian (si-bas-chun)
Sycorax (sik-uh-raks)
Trinculo (trin-kyoo-loh)

Scenes

A ship at sea and an island.

The Tempest

ACT I
Scene 1

Ship's deck.

(From backstage come storm noises—cracks of thunder, rain pouring, waves, etc. Characters portraying the sea run across the stage, carrying blue silky fabric over their heads.)

(ENTER ARIEL, quickly crossing the stage and holding a large model ship in his or her arms—if available—and making it swoop and dive as if it is tossed on the ocean.)

(In this scene, there should be a building sense of chaos and panic— the characters are afraid their ship will split and they will drown. All the action should happen swiftly.)

(Loud cries of sailors can be heard from backstage.)

(ENTER NARRATOR.)

NARRATOR:
Welcome to our production of *The Tempest*. This is Shakespeare's last play, and it has the same power to charm audiences today as it did in 1610 or 1611, when it was first performed. *The Tempest* has it all: a shipwreck, a deserted island, airy spirits, and a lowly monster. Our play also has magic and romance, treachery and forgiveness.

BACKSTAGE VOICES:
—Fall to it!
—Bestir yourselves! Bestir!
—Fall to it!
—Take in the topsail!

(ENTER SHIPMASTER and BOATSWAIN.)

MASTER:
Boatswain!

BOATSWAIN:
Here master, what cheer?

MASTER:

Speak to the mariners. Fall to it or we run ourselves aground. Bestir! Bestir!

(EXIT MASTER and BOATSWAIN.)

(ENTER MARINERS.)

BOATSWAIN:

Heigh, my hearts! Cheerly, cheerly, my hearts! Yare, yare! Take in the topsail. Tend to the master's whistle. Blow, till thou burst thy wind.

(ENTER ALONSO, SEBASTIAN, ANTONIO, FERDINAND, and GONZALO.)

ALONSO:

Good boatswain, have care. Where's the master?

ANTONIO:

Where's the master, boatswain?

BOATSWAIN:

Go below! Keep to your cabins!

GONZALO:

Good fellow, be patient. Pray remember whom thou dost have on board—the King of Naples and the Duke of Milan!

BOATSWAIN:

Sir, I have no one on board that I love more than myself. If you can command these elements to silence, do so now! If you cannot, give thanks you have lived so long. Cheerly, good hearts! Out of our way, I say!

(These CHARACTERS EXIT then RE-ENTER, as passengers and sailors cross back and forth across the ship.)

BOATSWAIN:

Yet again? What do you here? Have you a mind to sink?

SEBASTIAN:

A pox on your throat, you bawling, blasphemous, incharitable dog!

ANTONIO:

You cur, you insolent noise-maker. We are less afraid to be drowned than you are.

(ENTER MARINERS, wet.)

MARINERS:

All lost! To prayers, to prayers! All lost!

BOATSWAIN:

What, must we drown?

(Loud noise.)

GONZALO:

We split! We split! Farewell, my wife and children! Farewell!
We split, we split, we split!

ANTONIO:

Let's all sink with the king.

SEBASTIAN:

Let's take leave of him.

(EXIT ANTONIO and SEBASTIAN.)

GONZALO:

Now would I give a thousand furlongs of sea for an acre of barren ground. The wills above be done! But I would fain die a dry death.

(EXIT ALL.)

ACT I
Scene 2

The island.

NARRATOR:

The shipwreck took place off the coast of a tiny desert island in the Mediterranean. Alonso, the King of Naples, and his brother Antonio, the Duke of Milan, are returning home from the king's daughter's wedding in Tunisia. A wild storm came up, threatening to drown them at sea. There are a handful of inhabitants on the island, but only the old man Prospero and his daughter Miranda are humans. The others are spirits or part spirits. Twelve years ago Prospero himself washed up on that island, along with Miranda, his daughter, who was barely three years old at the time. You will soon learn who Prospero is and where he is from.

(In front of Prospero's "poor cell." Can be represented by a hut, a tent, or a curtain.)

(ENTER PROSPERO and MIRANDA. Prospero carries his mantle or magic cloak over his arm.)

MIRANDA:

My dearest father, if you and your art has put the wild waters
In this roar, calm them.
O, I have suffered with those I saw suffer!
A brave vessel who had, no doubt, a noble creature in her,
Dashed all to pieces. Poor souls, they perished!

PROSPERO:

Be collected. No more amazement.
Tell your pitying heart
there is no harm done.

MIRANDA:

Oh!

PROSPERO:

I have done nothing but in care of thee, my dear one.
Of you, who are ignorant of who you really are
And where we come from.

MIRANDA:

Knowing more has never troubled my thoughts.

PROSPERO:

(Lays down his magic cloak.)
Lie there, my art. Daughter, wipe thine eyes.
I have ordered the wreck you have just seen,
which touched your compassion so.
But no soul is harmed. And now the hour has come
For you to know who you are
And that I am better than what you see.

MIRANDA:

You have often begun to tell me what I am, but stopped.

PROSPERO:

Can you remember a time before we came here? You were but three years old.

MIRANDA:

Certainly I can, but 'tis far off and rather like a dream.
Had I not four or five women who tended me?

PROSPERO:

That you did and more, but come, sit down and I will tell you . . .

(Prospero and Miranda move aside, sit down, and he talks to her quietly as Narrator speaks.)

NARRATOR:

Prospero tells Miranda an amazing story. All she has ever known is this island and their simple life on it. What Prospero tells her is that twelve years ago he was the Duke of Milan in Italy. His wife had died, leaving him with the infant Miranda. Prospero was a kind duke and his people loved him, but he spent most of his time studying and learning about things like magic and astrology. Meanwhile his power-hungry brother Antonio plotted with the King of Naples to seize the dukedom for himself.

PROSPERO:

Dost thou hear?

MIRANDA:

(Standing up and moving forward, for emphasis.)
I do, Father. Your tale, sir, would cure deafness.

PROSPERO:

Tell me, if this does sound like a brother.
The King of Naples was my enemy.
He agreed to remove me from the dukedom.
Antonio opened the gates of Milan one midnight
And hurried us through them—me and your crying self.

MIRANDA:

Alack, for pity! Why did they not destroy us?

PROSPERO:

Well asked, daughter. Hear a little further.
So great was the love my people bore me
My brother dared not put so bloody a mark on the business.
They took us out to sea and left us in a rotten carcass of a tub—
No tackle, sail, nor mast, and even the rats had left it.

MIRANDA:

Alack, what trouble was I then to you!

PROSPERO:

O, no, you were a cherub that did preserve me with your smiles.

MIRANDA:

How came we ashore?

PROSPERO:

Sit and I will tell you more.

(They sit.)

NARRATOR:

Prospero tells Miranda that a wise and kind friend, Gonzalo, sent with them not only food and fresh water but also a good quantity of clothes, linen, and other necessities. He also sent many books from Prospero's beloved library. What Prospero does NOT tell Miranda yet is who was on that fine sea vessel she just saw tossed in the wild storm. The boat carried the evil Antonio, King Alonso, and the good Gonzalo. Prospero used his magic to bring about the storm and cast their broken ship upon these shores. Miranda will learn the truth soon.

(Miranda leans back or moves to the floor and lies down. Prospero waves his hand over her head, as if casting a spell over her.)

PROSPERO:

Thou art inclined to sleep. Give it way. *(Claps his hands, calls out.)*
Spirit, come. I am ready now.
Approach, my Ariel, come.

(ENTER ARIEL, "flying" or running—he should enter and exit with some distinctive movement and MUSIC to show that he is an airy creature not of this world.)

ARIEL:

All hail, great master! Grave sir, hail! I come
To answer thy best pleasure, be it to fly,
To swim, to dive into the fire, to ride
On the curled clouds.

PROSPERO:

You have performed exactly the tempest I bade thee.

ARIEL:

To every point.
All but the mariners plunged into the foaming brine
And quit the vessel.

PROSPERO:

Why, that's my spirit! But are they safe, Ariel?

ARIEL:

Not a hair perished, and their garments fresher than before.
I have dispersed them about the isle.

PROSPERO:

Ariel, there is more work.

ARIEL:

Is there more toil? Master, remember what thou hast promised to me.

PROSPERO:

How now, Moody? What is it thou demands?

ARIEL:

My liberty. I have done thee worthy service.
Thou did promise to free me after one full year.

PROSPERO:

Do not forget what a torment I did free you from.

ARIEL:

I do not forget, sir. I was enslaved by the foul witch Sycorax
And after she died, by Caliban, her son.

PROSPERO:

A dull thing, who I now keep in service.
When I arrived to free you, your groans did make wolves howl.

ARIEL:

I thank thee, master. I will do thy bidding gently.

PROSPERO:

Do so, and after two days, I will discharge thee.

ARIEL:

That's my noble master!

PROSPERO:

Go make thyself a nymph of the sea,
Invisible to every eye but yours and mine. Go!

(EXIT ARIEL.)

PROSPERO:

(Abruptly clapping his hands.)
Awake, dear heart! Thou hast slept well.

MIRANDA:

(Stretching.)
The strangeness of your story put heaviness in me.

PROSPERO:

Shake it off. We'll go to visit Caliban, my slave.

MIRANDA:

'Tis a villain, sir, I do not love to look on.

PROSPERO:

Yet he does make our fire and fetch in our wood.
What, ho, Caliban! Come forth, tortoise!

The Tempest

(ENTER CALIBAN. He can crawl or slither. He can be hunchbacked or strangely contorted, human and monster at the same time.)

183

CALIBAN:

(Resentfully.)
A southwest wind blow on you
And blister you all over.
When you first came here to my island, you made much of me,
Gave me water with berries in it. And then I loved you and
Showed you all the qualities of the island—
The fresh springs, the salt pits. Cursed be that I did so!
Now I am chained to this hard rock.

PROSPERO:

Thou most lying slave. I treated you with human kindness
Till you showed violence to me and my child. Therefore
Are you confined to this rock.
Go, hence! Fetch us fuel and be quick.

CALIBAN:

You taught me language, and so I know how to curse.
The red plague rid you
For learning me your language!

(EXIT CALIBAN, followed by PROSPERO and MIRANDA.)

NARRATOR:

Caliban was the only humanlike inhabitant of the island when Prospero and Miranda first came there. Prospero did treat him well at first. Later, he forced Caliban to be his slave when the creature became violent, and it was obvious Prospero couldn't trust him.

And now Ferdinand appears—the son of King Alonso. He believes that everyone else on the ship has perished and that he alone has washed up on this island. When Miranda first sees the young man, she is charmed. Her father and Caliban are the only other human forms she has seen in twelve years. Ferdinand is equally fascinated.

(MUSIC. ENTER ARIEL, strumming a mandolin or other stringed instrument. Song recorded or sung by Ariel, as written for the original play.)

Full fathom five thy father lies.
Of his bones are coral made.
Those are pearls that were his eyes.
Nothing of him that doth fade
But doth suffer a sea change
Into something rich and strange.
Sea nymphs hourly ring his knell.
Hark, now I hear them: ding dong bell.

(ENTER FERDINAND, who can't see Ariel, but looks around as if for the source of the music.)

FERDINAND:

Where should this music be? In the air or the earth?

MIRANDA:

What is it? A spirit?
Lord, how it looks about!
I might call him a thing divine!

FERDINAND:

(Seeing them and instantly falling in love with Miranda.)
Oh, wonder! Be you a maid or a goddess?

MIRANDA:

No wonder, sir. But certainly a maid.

FERDINAND:

My own language! Were I only in the place where this language is spoken. My father the king of Naples, and all his lords did perish in the sea and I do weep for them.

MIRANDA:

Alack, for mercy!

PROSPERO:

(Aside to the audience.) At the first sight, they see with the eyes of love.
Delicate Ariel, I'll set you free for this.
But this business must not be so swift.
I must make it harder for them
Lest the prize be too easy in the winning.
(Crossing stage to Ferdinand and Miranda.)
Do you take the name of one who you are not?
Have you put yourself on this island as a spy,
To win it from me?

MIRANDA:

Why does my father speak so ungently?

PROSPERO:

Speak you not for him. He is a traitor.

MIRANDA:

He is gentle and not fearful.

PROSPERO:

What! Put thy sword up, traitor! I can disarm you with this stick.

MIRANDA:

I beseech you!

PROSPERO:

Hang not on my garments. Silence!
One word more shall make me punish you.
Thou thinkst there is no better shape than he?
Why, next to most men, this is a monster like Caliban
And they to him are angels.

MIRANDA:

Then I have no ambition to see a goodlier man.

FERDINAND:

My spirits are all bound up, as in a dream.
My father's loss, the weakness which I feel.

Even this man's threats are but light to me.
If I can behold this maid once a day from my prison,
Space enough have I.

PROSPERO:

(Aside.) It works, the charm works.
He loves her.
(To Ferdinand.) Come, follow me, sir.

MIRANDA:

Be of comfort.
My father is of a better nature, sir,
Than he appears now.

PROSPERO:

(To Ariel.) Thou shalt be as free as mountain winds.
Just do all points of my command.

ARIEL:

To the syllable.

(EXIT ALL.)

ACT II
Scene 1

Other side of the island.

(ENTER KING ALONSO, SEBASTIAN, ANTONIO, GONZALO, and noblemen ADRIAN and FRANCISCO, as Narrator is speaking.)

NARRATOR:

King Alonso is alive and so are the rest of his fellow travelers, but he is sure that his son Ferdinand is gone forever. Gonzalo means well and tries to comfort him, but everyone finds Gonzalo tiresome and annoying. Sebastian and Antonio mock him for being so talkative. However, Sebastian and Antonio have more on their minds than making fun of Gonzalo.

GONZALO:

Beseech you, sir, be merry. You have cause—
So do we all—of joy. For our escape
Is worth more than our loss.
Our woe is common. Every day

Some sailor's wife and the masters of a merchant ship
Have just our theme of woe.
Wisely, good sir, weigh our sorrow with our comfort.

KING ALONSO:

(Exasperated.)
Pray thee, peace.

SEBASTIAN:

(To Antonio.) Antonio, look how Gonzalo is winding up
the watch of his wit!
By and by it will strike.

ANTONIO:

Fie, Sebastian, what a spendthrift he is with his tongue.

(Antonio and Sebastian laugh mockingly at Gonzalo.)

GONZALO:

Therefore, my lord—

ALONSO:

I pray thee, peace!

GONZALO:

Here is everything we need for life!
How lush the grass looks!
How green! But the rarity of it is—

(Sebastian is laughing, nudging Antonio.)

GONZALO:

. . . As I say, the rarity of it is that our garments that were drenched in
the sea seem now as fresh as when we were in Tunis at the marriage of your
daughter, who is now queen.

KING ALONSO:

O, you cram these words in to mine ears against
The stomach of my sense! Would I had never
Married my daughter there, for coming thence
My son is lost! O, my son and heir
Of Naples and Milan, what strange fish
Hath made his meal on thee?

FRANCISCO:

Sir, he may live.

I saw him beat the waves under him
And ride upon their backs.
I do not doubt he came alive to land.

KING ALONSO:

No, no, he's gone.

GONZALO:

(Gently, to Alonso.)
It is foul weather in us all, good sir.
When you are cloudy.

KING ALONSO:

Prithee, no more.

(ENTER ARIEL, who is always invisible to them. MUSIC.)

(Antonio and Sebastian still laughing with each other at Gonzalo's expense.)

GONZALO:

Will you laugh me asleep? For I am very heavy.

(Everyone falls asleep except Alonso, Antonio, and Sebastian.)

KING ALONSO:

What, all so soon asleep? I wish my thoughts would
Shut up with my eyes.

SEBASTIAN:

Please you, sir, do not refuse the offer of sleep.
It is a comforter.

ANTONIO:

We two, my lord,
Will guard your person while you take your rest.

(Alonso sleeps. EXIT ARIEL.)

SEBASTIAN:

What a strange drowsiness possesses them!

ANTONIO:

They dropped as by a thunderstroke.
What might, worthy Sebastian, what might . . . ?
Oh, no, no more.
And yet methinks I see in thy face

What thou shouldst be.
My strong imagination sees a crown
Dropping upon thy head.

SEBASTIAN:

Say on.

ANTONIO:

Thus, sir. The king's son is not alive—'tis impossible.

SEBASTIAN:

I have no hope
That he's undrowned.

ANTONIO:

And out of that no hope
What great hope have you! Tell me,
Who is the next heir of Naples?

SEBASTIAN:

The king's daughter, Claribel.

ANTONIO:

And she is Queen of Tunis dwelling in far-off Africa,
Ten leagues beyond man's life.
Do you understand me?

SEBASTIAN:

Methinks I do. I remember
You did supplant your brother Prospero.

ANTONIO:

And look how well my garments sit upon me.
Listen, now—

(Antonio pulls Sebastian aside and talks to him privately.)

NARRATOR:

You might think that Antonio would simply be grateful for being alive rather than drowned in a fierce and deadly storm. Instead, he is plotting and scheming. Antonio tells Sebastian his wicked plan. He says that he will kill the king, and he directs Sebastian to kill Gonzalo at the same time. Then, between the two of them, they will be King of Milan and Duke of Naples and have the power of Italy just about sewn up. But at the moment Sebastian and Antonio raise their swords to kill Gonzalo and the king, Ariel's hidden magic causes King Alonso and his loyal friend to wake from their sleep.

(Sebastian and Antonio move toward the sleeping king and Gonzalo, drawing their swords.)

(MUSIC.)

(ENTER ARIEL, invisible to all onstage. Ariel bends and whispers in Gonzalo's ear.)

GONZALO:

Now, good angels preserve the king!

(Gonzalo wakes Alonso.)

ALONSO:

Why, how now, ho!
(To Sebastian.) Awake? Why is your sword drawn?

SEBASTIAN:

While we stood here guarding you
We heard a hollow burst of bellowing
Like bulls, or rather lions. Did it not wake you?

ANTONIO:

Oh, 'twas a din to fright a monster's ear.
Sure, it was the roar of a whole herd of lions.

ALONSO:

I heard nothing. Hear you this, Gonzalo?

GONZALO:

Upon mine honor, sir, I heard a humming,
Which did awake me.
I shaked you, sir, and cried out. As mine eyes opened,
I saw their weapons drawn.

ALONSO:

Lead off this ground and let's make further search
For my poor son.

ARIEL:

(Aside, toward the audience.)
Prospero my lord shall know what I have done.
So, King, go safely on to seek thy son.

(EXIT ALL, with Ariel following the others.)

ACT II
Scene 2

Other side of island.

(ENTER CALIBAN with a load of wood.)

CALIBAN:
All the infections that the sun sucks up
Should fall on Prospero and make him
Inch by inch a disease!
Lo, now, lo! Here comes a spirit to torment me
For bringing in wood too slowly!

(Caliban quickly lies down, covers himself with his cloak, blanket, or shirt.)

NARRATOR:
Caliban knows that Prospero controls the spirits on the island, and he complains that Prospero has set them all against him. Goblins chase him and mock him and bite him, he says. He stumbles on hedgehogs, and his legs are wound about with snakes. Caliban is a disagreeable character and he doesn't have a friend in the world. In this scene, he is about to meet two foolish servants who have washed up on shore with the royal party.

(ENTER TRINCULO.)

TRINCULO:
There is neither bush nor shrub and here is another storm brewing. If it should thunder like it did before, I know not where to hide my head. *(He sees Caliban.)* What have we here? Man or fish? Dead or alive? Smells like a fish. Ahhh! Alas, the storm is come again. Ahhh! There is no other shelter. Ahhh!

(Trinculo crawls under Caliban's cloak, his head to Caliban's feet.)

(ENTER STEPHANO, carrying a bottle and obviously drunk.)

STEPHANO:
(Singing tunelessly.)
I shall no more to sea, to sea,
Here shall I die ashore.
This is a scurvy tune. But here's my comfort. *(Drinks.)*

CALIBAN:

Do not torment me! O!

STEPHANO:

What's the matter? Have we devils here?

CALIBAN:

The spirit torments me. O!

STEPHANO:

This is some monster of the isle with four legs, who has got the fever. Where the devil should he learn our language? If I can tame him and bring him to Naples, he's a present for any emperor.

CALIBAN:

Do not torment me, prithee. I'll bring my wood home faster.

STEPHANO:

He's in a fit now and does not talk the wisest. He shall taste of my bottle. Come, here is something that will give language to a cat. Open your mouth. This will shake your shaking.

(Caliban drinks.)

TRINCULO:

I should know that voice. It should be—but Stephano is drowned and these are devils! O, defend me!

STEPHANO:

Four legs and two voices—come, I will pour some in thy other mouth.

TRINCULO:

Stephano!

STEPHANO:

Does thy other mouth call me? Mercy, mercy!

(The two of them scuffle, and eventually Trinculo emerges from under the cloak.)

TRINCULO:

You are not drowned!
(He spins Stephano around in delight.)

(Caliban crawls out and stares at Stephano.)

CALIBAN:

These be fine things, if they be not sprites.

(Bows, says to Stephano.)
I'll swear upon that bottle to be thy true subject.

STEPHANO:

How did thou escape?

TRINCULO:

I swam ashore, man, like a duck. *(Drinks.)*
Have you any more of this?

STEPHANO:

My cellar is in a rock by the seaside, where my wine is hid.

CALIBAN:

Hast thou dropped from heaven?

STEPHANO:

Out of the moon, I do assure thee.

CALIBAN:

I'll show thee every fertile inch of the island, and I will kiss thy foot.
I pray thee, be my god.

STEPHANO:

Come on, then. Down, and swear.

(Caliban kneels.)

TRINCULO:

I shall laugh myself to death at this puppy-headed monster.

CALIBAN:

I'll show thee the best springs. I'll pluck thee berries.
I'll fish for thee and get thee wood enough.
A plague upon the tyrant that I serve. I'll follow thee,
My wondrous man.

TRINCULO:

A most ridiculous monster, to make a wonder of a poor drunkard.

CALIBAN:

Let me bring thee where crabs grow,
To clustering filberts. Sometimes I'll get thee
Young seabirds from the rock. Wilt thou go with me?

STEPHANO:

I pray thee, lead the way without any more talking.

CALIBAN:

(*Singing.*)

'Ban, 'Ban, Caliban! Caliban has a new master.

Freedom, high-day! High-day, freedom!

STEPHANO:

O brave monster! Lead the way.

(*EXIT ALL.*)

ACT III
Scene 1

(*ENTER FERDINAND, staggering under the weight of several logs.*)

FERDINAND:

This task would be heavy to me,

But my sweet mistress makes my labors pleasure.

O, she is ten times more gentle than her father is harsh!

I must remove thousands of these logs and pile them up.

But sweet thoughts of her do refresh my labor.

(*ENTER MIRANDA. ENTER PROSPERO, back of stage, unseen by Ferdinand.*)

MIRANDA:

Work not so hard, sir!

I'll bear your logs a while.

Pray, give me that.

 I'll carry it to the pile.

FERDINAND:

No, precious creature,

I would rather break my back

Than you should undergo such dishonor

While I sit lazy by.

MIRANDA:

You look wearily.

FERDINAND:

No, noble mistress, 'tis fresh morning with me

When you are by at night. I do beg you

So that I may say it in my prayers—What is your name?

MIRANDA:

Miranda. —O my father,
I have broke your command to say so!

FERDINAND:

Admired Miranda!
You are so perfect and so peerless. You are created
Of every creature's best.

MIRANDA:

I have seen no woman's face
But mine own in the glass. Nor have I seen
More men than you, good friend,
And my dear father.

FERDINAND:

I am a prince, Miranda. I do think I am a king now—
I wish it were not so. I wouldn't endure this servitude
But that the very instant I saw you
My heart flew to your service and made me slave to it.

MIRANDA:

Do you love me?

FERDINAND:

O earth, bear witness to this sound.
Beyond all limit of what else in the world I do love,
I love, prize, honor you.

PROSPERO:

(Aside.) Fair encounter of two most rare affections.

FERDINAND:

Wherefore weep you?

MIRANDA:

At mine unworthiness.
I am your wife if you will marry me.

FERDINAND:

Here's my hand.

MIRANDA:

And mine. And now farewell
'Til half an hour hence.

(EXIT MIRANDA and FERDINAND. EXIT PROSPERO, following them.)

NARRATOR:

Prospero is very pleased with how things are working out. It looks as though his daughter will soon be married to the future King of Naples. Meanwhile, Caliban and his new friends are setting up the drunken Stephano to be king of the island.

ACT III
Scene 2

(ENTER STEPHANO, TRINCULO, and CALIBAN, all tipsy.)

STEPHANO:

My man monster has drowned his tongue in drink.
Speak Monsieur Monster!

CALIBAN:

How does thy Honor? Let me lick thy shoe.
Thou shalt be lord of the island and I'll serve thee.

(ENTER ARIEL, invisible to them.)

STEPHANO:

How now shall this come about?

CALIBAN:

I'll lead thee to Prospero when he is asleep, my lord.
And you can knock a nail into his head.
First seize his books of magic,
Then batter his skull or punch him with a stake
Or cut his windpipe with thy knife.
Save his daughter—she is beautiful.
But remember to burn his magic books,
For without them he's but a sot, as I am.

STEPHANO:

Monster, I will kill this man. His daughter and I will be king and queen. Save our Graces! You and Trinculo shall be viceroys. Dost thou like the plot, Trinculo?

TRINCULO:

Excellent.

ARIEL:

(Aside to the audience.) This will I tell my master.

STEPHANO:

Come on, Trinculo, let us sing! *(Sings tunelessly.)*
Flout 'em and count 'em
And scout 'em and flout 'em
Thought is free.

(MUSIC. Ariel plays or hums the tune, and they all look frightened. They can hear him, but they can't see him.)

STEPHANO:

What is this? *(To the invisible MUSIC.)* If thou be a man, show thyself. If thou be a devil, take it as thou will.

CALIBAN:

Be not afeard. The island is full of noises,
Sounds and sweet airs that give delight and hurt not.

STEPHANO:

Lead, monster. We'll follow.

(EXIT CALIBAN, TRINCULO, and STEPHANO.)

ACT III
Scene 3

(ENTER KING ALONSO, SEBASTIAN, ANTONIO, GONZALO, ADRIAN, and FRANCISCO, limping and exhausted, breathing hard. ENTER PROSPERO, invisible to them.)

NARRATOR:

Things are not going so well for the royal party, as they are weary, thirsty, and hungry. They have been searching for Ferdinand without success.

GONZALO:

By your leave, I must needs rest me.

KING ALONSO:

Sit down, old lord. Even here I will put off my hope. He is drowned, and the sea mocks our search. Let him go.

ANTONIO:

(Aside to Sebastian.) I am glad he is out of hope.

SEBASTIAN:

Let us take the next advantage—tonight.

(MUSIC. ENTER SPIRITS, dressed strangely, carrying in a banquet. They gently and graciously invite the weary travelers to come eat.)

KING ALONSO:

Heaven send us guardian angels! What are these?

GONZALO:

If in Naples I should report this,
Would they believe me?
Their manners are more gentle and kind
Than some of our human generation.

PROSPERO:

(Aside.) Honest lord, thou says well.
Some of you there are worse than devils.

(MUSIC. The spirits dance around and continue beckoning the others to the feast. Then SPIRITS EXIT.)

(King Alonso and the others move toward the food. They are not sure whether or not to eat it. Just as they are about to reach for something, there is a loud sound—crash of thunder, pounding, or some other sound that frightens them. ARIEL ENTERS, dressed like a harpy—face of a woman, wings and talons of a bird. The men raise their swords as if to attack the creature.)

ARIEL:

(In disguise.) You three from Milan did overthrow good Prospero, and expose him unto the sea with his innocent child. For this the powers have not forgotten you and have incensed the sea against you. They have taken your son from you, Alonso, and condemned him to a lingering perdition worse than death.

(The men look terrified. MUSIC. SPIRITS ENTER, dancing, then take away the food and EXIT.)

PROSPERO:

(Aside.) My charms work,
Mine enemies are all knit up in their distractions.

They are now in my power and in these fits I leave them.
I will visit young Ferdinand, whom they suppose is drowned, and
I will leave our darling.

(EXIT PROSPERO.)

KING ALONSO:

O, monstrous, monstrous!

(EXIT KING ALONSO.)

SEBASTIAN:

One fiend at a time we'll fight.

(EXIT SEBASTIAN and ANTONIO.)

GONZALO:

All three of them are desperate. Their great guilt
Like poison working years after the crime.
Follow them swiftly
And keep them from whatever this madness may bring them to.

(EXIT GONZALO, ADRIAN, and FRANCISCO.)

ACT IV
Scene 1

(ENTER PROSPERO, FERDINAND, and MIRANDA.)

PROSPERO:

Ferdinand, I have austerely punished you
As a trial of thy love for my daughter and
You have wondrously stood the test.
Here before Heaven
I reward you with her hand. You may marry.

FERDINAND:

(Bowing.) I hope for quiet days, fair issue, and long life.

PROSPERO:

Sit then and talk with her. She is thine own.

(Ferdinand and Miranda clasp hands and move aside to sit and talk quietly.)

(Prospero looks around, calls "Ariel!" and ARIEL ENTERS. Prospero gives silent instructions to Ariel, who then EXITS.)

NARRATOR:

Prospero will soon set Ariel free, but for a little while longer he needs Ariel's connection to the spirit world. Now that he has granted permission for Ferdinand to marry Miranda, he wants the magical spirits to help them celebrate.

(ENTER IRIS the rainbow, messenger of the gods and goddesses, dancing about the stage. She could wave a rainbow-colored silky scarf or wear a multicolored dress, leotard, etc.)

NARRATOR:

Iris is symbolized by her rainbow colors. She is a messenger from the other world—the world of gods and goddesses. Juno, Queen of the Sky, has asked Iris to come here and call forth Ceres, goddess of the rich earth. They will all celebrate the love and marriage of Ferdinand and Miranda.

(ENTER CERES, goddess of the earth. Could carry large bunch of dried flowers, tied up and/or fruit to symbolize earth.)

(ENTER JUNO, with symbolic crown.)

(MUSIC.)

JUNO:

I am Juno, Queen of the Sky.
Honor, riches, marriage—blessing
Long continuance, and increasing,
Hourly joys be still upon you.
Juno sings her blessings on you.

FERDINAND:

This is a most majestic vision.
Are these spirits?

PROSPERO:

Spirits, which by my art
I have called to enact my present fancies.

FERDINAND:

Let me live here ever!

(Spirits dance around. MORE SPIRITS, nymphs, if available, ENTER and dance, preferably with MUSIC.)

NARRATOR:

Right in the middle of the celebration, Prospero suddenly remembers the conspiracy against his life by the drunken Trinculo, Stephano, and Caliban.

(Prospero abruptly claps his hands loudly, looking impatient and angry. Music stops. EXIT ALL SPIRITS.)

PROSPERO:

I had forgot that foul conspiracy
Against my life by that beast Caliban
And his confederates.
Well done. No more.

MIRANDA:

Never to this day saw I my father so touched with anger.

PROSPERO:

Our revels now are ended.
These spirits are melted into air—into thin air.
The wonders of this world all will fade
Like this insubstantial pageant, leaving nothing behind.
We are such stuff as dreams are made on
And our little life
Is rounded with sleep.
Go, be cheerful. Rest, and wait for me.

FERDINAND:

We wish you peace.

(EXIT FERDINAND and MIRANDA.)

(ENTER ARIEL.)

PROSPERO:

Spirit, where did you leave Caliban and those rascals?

ARIEL:

Sir, they were red-hot with drinking.
I charmed their ears and led them through briers,
Pricking gorse, and thorns. At last I left them
In that foul lake beyond your cell
Dancing up to their chins.

(ENTER CALIBAN, TRINCULO, and STEPHANO wearing wet clothes, if possible, and with wet hair. They cannot see Prospero and Ariel.)

CALIBAN:

See thou here. You approach his cell. No noise! And enter.
Do that good mischief which may make this island
Your own forever, and I, thy Caliban,
Forever thy foot-licker.

(The three tiptoe across stage. They peer offstage, as if they are looking into Prospero's closet or see his clothes hanging on a line.).

TRINCULO:

O King Stephano! Worthy Stephano! Look what a wardrobe is here for thee!

CALIBAN:

Let it alone, thou fool. Do the murder first!

(Loud, frightening noises to represent dangerous wild-animal spirits. ENTER SPIRITS in masks, or otherwise disguised and chase the three around the stage. Prospero and Ariel observe this whole scene, then nod at each other and EXIT.)

NARRATOR:

At this point all of Prospero's enemies are at his mercy. Soon his labors will end and Ariel will be set free. In the meantime, he has some business with his brother Antonio and with King Alonso. He will release them from their charmed state and confront them. At the beginning of the last act of our play, Ariel tells Prospero to have pity on his brother and the king, and Prospero says that he does have pity for them—and he forgives them.

ACT V
Scene 1

(ENTER PROSPERO in his magic cloak and ARIEL.)

(ENTER MIRANDA and FERDINAND, who sit off to side playing chess. They remain unseen by other characters until later in the scene.)

PROSPERO:

How fares the king and his followers?

ARIEL:

If you beheld them now, your affections for your brother and the king would become tender. Mine would, if I were human.

PROSPERO:

And mine shall. Their high wrongs did strike me to the quick—
Yet, the rarer action is in virtue, not in vengeance.
Go, release them, Ariel.

(EXIT ARIEL.)

(Prospero traces a huge circle with his staff.)

PROSPERO:

I have made dim
The noontide sun, called forth the mutinous winds.
I have given fire to the dread rattling thunder.
But this rough magic I now put aside.

*(ARIEL ENTERS. ENTER KING ALONSO, GONZALO, SEBASTIAN,
ANTONIO, ADRIAN, and FRANCISCO. They all look dazed, dejected, as
they stand within the circle Prospero has just made.)*

PROSPERO:

Not one of them that looks on me would yet know me.
O good Gonzalo, my true preserver.
I will send you home.
Alonso, most cruelly you did use me and my daughter
Thy brother was a partner in the act.
Antonio, you, brother mine, who entertained ambition
Would here have killed your king. I do forgive thee,
unnatural though you are.
Ariel—fetch me the hat and sword in my cell.
Quickly, spirit,
You shall soon be free.

*(ARIEL EXITS, quickly RE-ENTERS with Prospero's robes from when he
was duke. Helps Prospero put on robes.)*

(MUSIC.)

ARIEL:

Where the bee sucks, there suck I.
In a cowslip's bell I lie,
There I couch when owls do cry.
On the bat's back I do fly

After summer merrily.
Merrily, merrily shall I live now
Under the blossom that hangs on the bow.

PROSPERO:

Why, that's my dainty Ariel. I shall miss
Thee, but yet thou shalt have freedom.

(EXIT ARIEL.)

PROSPERO:

So, so, so.
To the king's ship. Wake the mariners and
Bring hither the master and the boatswain.

GONZALO:

All torment, trouble, wonder, and amazement inhabits here.
Heaven guide us out of this fearful country.

(Prospero steps forward and suddenly they all see him and look amazed and dazed, rubbing their eyes.)

PROSPERO:

Behold, sir king,
The wronged Duke of Milan, Prospero.
(Prospero embraces Alonso.)
To thee and thy company I bid
A hearty welcome.

ALONSO:

This must be a most strange story.
Thy dukedom I relinquish to you and do beg
Thou pardon me my wrongs. But how should
Prospero be living and be here?

PROSPERO:

(To Gonzalo.) First, noble friend,
Let me embrace thine age,
Whose honor cannot be measured or confined.
(To Antonio.) For you, most wicked sir, I do forgive
Thy rankest fault, all of them, and require
My dukedom of thee.

KING ALONSO:

If thou be Prospero,
Give us particulars of thy preservation,
And how thou hast met us here where I have lost
My dear son Ferdinand.

PROSPERO:

And I am woe for it, sir. I have lost my daughter.

ALONSO:

Thy daughter!
O heavens, that they were living both in Naples,
The king and queen there!

PROSPERO:

No more yet of this,
For 'tis a chronicle of day by day.
Welcome, sir. Look in here, and I will
Acquaint you with as good a thing as my dukedom is to me.

(Prospero pulls curtain or screen aside to indicate his cell and shows him Ferdinand and Miranda, sitting and playing chess.)

MIRANDA:

Sweet lord, you play me false.

FERDINAND:

No, my dearest love, I would not for the world.

(Ferdinand and King Alonso see each other, amazed.)

SEBASTIAN:

A most high miracle!

ALONSO:

Now, all the blessings of a glad father encompass you!

MIRANDA:

O wonder!
How many goodly creatures are there here!
How beauteous mankind is! O, brave new world
That has such people in it!

KING ALONSO:

Come aside and tell me, who is this maid with whom thou wast at play.

(They move off and talk.)

GONZALO:

Look down, you gods
And on this couple drop a blessed crown.

(ENTER ARIEL, with SHIP'S MASTER and BOATSWAIN.)

BOATSWAIN:

Now we have safely found
Our king and company. Our ship,
Which was split but three hours since,
Is tight and seaworthy, bravely rigged as when
We first put out to sea.

(Prospero looks at Ariel, approvingly. Ariel bows.)

ARIEL:

(To Prospero.) Sir, all this service have I done since I went.

(EXIT ARIEL.)

ALONSO:

This is as strange a maze as ever men trod.

(RE-ENTER ARIEL with CALIBAN, TRINCULO, and STEFANO.)

ALONSO:

Is this not Stephano, my drunken butler?

SEBASTIAN:

He is drunk now. Where had he wine?

ALONSO:

And Trinculo is reeling ripe! Where should they
Find this grand liquor?
How came thou in this pickle?

(Alonso gestures to Caliban.)

And this is as strange a thing as ever I looked on.

PROSPERO:

He is as disproportioned in his manners
As in his shape. *(To Caliban.)* Go to, away!

(EXIT CALIBAN, followed by STEPHANO and TRINCULO.)

PROSPERO:

Sir, I invite your Highness and your train
To my poor cell.

ALONSO:

I long to hear the story of your life.

PROSPERO:

I'll deliver all.

(He starts to walk away with King Alonso and the others following.)

NARRATOR:

Prospero invites the royal party to stay the night, and he promises to tell King Alonso everything. He plans to join them on their ship, which has been restored to perfect condition by Ariel's magic, and all of them will set sail for Naples.

PROSPERO:

Calm seas, auspicious gales, and sail so expeditious—
(To Ariel.) My Ariel, chick, that is thy charge.
Then to the elements be free, and fare thou well.
Please you, draw near.

(EXIT ALL.)

NARRATOR:

It is the very end of our play. Prospero is simply a man now—not a magician. He has been wronged, but he forgives. He will allow his daughter to marry Ferdinand, so long as he knows she will be happy. He is ready to leave the island and return home to his dukedom. But first he comes onstage one more time. He addresses the audience as if he knows his job has been to entertain them. "Release me from my bands," he says, "with the help of your good hands." In other words, he tells the audience, if they approve of his story, they should clap and he will be set free.

(ENTER PROSPERO. He stands in the center front of stage, arms at his sides, addressing the audience. If his speech is too long, he can read it— or part of it—as long as he looks out at the audience.)

PROSPERO:

Now my charms are all o'erthrown,
And what strength I have's mine own,
Which is most faint. Now 'tis true
I must be here confined by you,
Or be sent to Naples. Let me not,
Since I have my dukedom got
And pardoned the deceiver, dwell
In this bare island by your spell,
But release me from my bands
With the help of your good hands.
Gentle breath of yours my sails
Must fill, or else my project fails,
Which was to please. Now I want
Spirits to enforce, art to enchant,
And my ending is despair,
Unless I be relieved by prayer,
Which pierces so that it assaults
Mercy itself, and frees all faults.
As you from crimes would pardoned be,
Let your indulgence set me free.

(EXIT PROSPERO.)

About Shakespeare

Who was William Shakespeare? Was he a scholar, a poet, an actor, a family man, an Elizabethan gentleman? Was he a genius? Was he even a real person, or is it possible someone else, or several people, created the literary masterpieces we attribute to him?

We know the answers to some of those questions. Shakespeare wasn't a scholar or a gentleman; he was a poet, a playwright, and an actor. He did have a family but lived apart from his wife and children for many years. He was a brilliant craftsman of the English language, surpassed by no one, so many would call him a genius. We don't really know at what age this talent showed itself. Shakespeare had a sound command of Latin grammar and literature, which he almost certainly learned at school, and he probably studied Greek there as well. He also knew a fair amount of history and was comfortable making observations about whatever were the commonly held notions of science and astrology in sixteenth-century England. These subjects he probably did not study at school but learned later on his own in London. Shakespeare's was not an elite education.

There are few details of Shakespeare's life. Apparently no one saw a reason to write them down, and Shakespeare himself left no diary or letters.

Records show William Shakespeare was born in April 1564 and baptized on April 26; and, as it was customary to baptize three or so days after birth, he was probably born on the twenty-third. He died fifty-two years later, in 1616, also in April. His parents were John Shakespeare, a glove maker and local government official, and Mary Arden; he was their eldest son and one of eight children.

We know that Shakespeare was married at nineteen and that less than nine months later he and his wife Anne Hathaway became parents of a daughter, Susanna. We also know that he left the small market town of Stratford sometime after his second two children (twins Hamnet and Judith) were born and made the trip to London, where he lived for the next twenty years, making only occasional trips back to Stratford.

Records exist of some of Shakespeare's London business dealings. In addition to producing a steady stream of plays and poetry, he was also part owner of several London theaters, and he was at least a minor actor in them as well. We know that much of his work was popular in his own lifetime, and he was considered a success in London theaters as well as at the courts of Queen Elizabeth I and King James I.

But did Shakespeare leave his home in Stratford because his marriage was unhappy or because he got a job as a traveling player? Did he leave because he knew he wanted to write plays and thought that London would be the best venue for them? Did he leave because he wanted a partnership in a new theater? Did his wife not accompany him to London with the children because she was from a Puritan family, and the Puritans disapproved of theater? All these are possibilities but not certainties.

The lives of modern writers are often written about and discussed because we readers want clues. We want to know if certain characters are the authors themselves or were inspired by their sisters or ex-husbands or grade-school teachers. Sometimes we're hoping that themes from the books will be explained by the authors' lives. Wanting to make these connections isn't wrong—it's human.

With some writers, though—both writers who died long ago and some scrupulously private modern writers—tapping these clues is not possible. We just don't know enough. Shakespeare's only son, Hamnet, died at age eleven and that sad fact might lend a special poignancy to the words of characters expressing sadness at the loss of children. On the other hand, Shakespeare certainly wrote of other life events with the same sensitivity. Shakespeare wrote knowledgeably about royalty and about the monarchy, but he was a commoner. He wrote about greed and passion and ambition, but we don't know for whom or what he felt those things. What we do know is more useful in the end: We know that his work is capable of inspiring us to think about ourselves. We can't use all that much from his life to explain his work, but we can use a lot from his work to explain and help us understand our own lives.

Was Shakespeare Shakespeare?

In the eighteenth century a thorny controversy started gathering steam suggesting that Shakespeare's work was not his own. The "Oxfordians" and other groups say that no one with William Shakespeare's inadequate education could have written all we say he did. Either a consortium of Oxford scholars created the plays and poems, or more likely, an Oxford University don named Edward da Vere wrote them.

This notion has been shot down by most serious Shakespeare scholars; and although it's entertaining and probably will continue to be floated as a possibility, the debate is useless. The "Stratfordians" maintain that William Shakespeare did write the work attributed to him (although a few early plays may have been collaborations), and that those who assume he could not have done so are elitists—products of a rigid English class system.

Not only did da Vere die before Shakespeare's last ten plays were written, but scholars tend to agree on several other pieces of evidence proving that Shakespeare penned his own plays. The First Folio of his plays was published in 1623, as a tribute to Shakespeare after his death, by two actors in his company. The poet Ben Jonson, who was both a rival and a friend, described Shakespeare's work as "not of an age, but for all time."

The Stratfordians say that there is no reason to assume that an Oxford don was more qualified to write for the stage than an experienced actor and writer. Shakespeare got plenty of preparation for his life's work.

True, this son of a local glove maker and small-town government official did not have a privileged upbringing, and he did not attend a university. He most likely attended the local grammar school in Stratford, which demanded that the (all-male) pupils spend six long days a week studying Latin language and literature, as well as Greek. Growing up in the country, he would have picked up some knowledge of the natural world, and he would have learned at least something of his father's trade.

Later, as a bright and ambitious young man living in London, Shakespeare learned history and literature on his own. He befriended other playwrights and poets, which would have enriched his writing. Writing and performing for the public gave him direct experience with what would and wouldn't work on the stage. Writing and performing for Queen Elizabeth taught him much about the monarchy and life at court.

Most important, though, Shakespeare had the qualities all truly great writers have: an uncommon facility for language, abundant curiosity, and a profound sensitivity to and understanding of human nature. And let's not forget one more essential ingredient in writing success: hard work. Shakespeare was only fifty-two when he died. In about twenty years of writing, he left us a legacy of more than forty plays, two popular lyric works, and 155 sonnets.

Shakespeare's Professional Life

By 1592 Shakespeare's work was very popular. It was produced often, and other playwrights and men of the stage mentioned him in their writings. He was a member of an acting company called Lord Chamberlain's Men, which became the King's Men after Queen Elizabeth's death and James I's accession to the throne in 1603. Lord Chamberlain's Men were associated with a couple of different theaters, the Globe and the Blackfriars, and Shakespeare both acted and wrote for the company.

Theater companies also traveled, particularly when the London theaters were forced to close because of disease or plague. Showing their plays to a wider audience was good publicity; and although it was the actors most audiences cheered for, not the writers, Shakespeare's plays were in demand.

Shakespeare never tried to publish his plays. It may not ever have occurred to him. He sold each play to the theater, after which the script became the theater's property. A number of Shakespeare's plays did appear in print during his lifetime, but these "bad quartos" were published by other people and were not sanctioned by Shakespeare. He probably didn't think of plays as literature but published his sonnets and his two long poems, "Venus and Adonis" and "The Rape of Lucrece," as a way to establish his reputation as a serious writer and make some more money.

After his death, two of Shakespeare's colleagues in the King's Men, John Heminges and Henry Condell, published a book of his plays called *Mr. William Shakespeares Comedies, Histories, & Tragedies. Published According to the True Originall Copies*. The First Folio, as it came to be known, brought together thirty-six plays by Shakespeare and wasn't particularly consistent or accurate in its editing or printing. The Second, Third, and Fourth Folios were subsequent editions published in the seventeenth century.

Approximate Chronological Order of Shakespeare's Plays

Shakespeare's plays are divided into comedies, histories, tragedies, and romances, with several of them straddling two categories. What follows is a complete list of Shakespeare's plays in approximate chronological order.

Love's Labour's Lost

King Henry VI, Part I

Titus Andronicus

The Comedy of Errors

King Henry VI, Part II

King Henry VI, Part III

The Taming of the Shrew

Two Gentlemen of Verona

King Richard III

King John

Romeo and Juliet

A Midsummer Night's Dream

King Richard II

The Merchant of Venice

King Henry IV, Part I

King Henry IV, Part II

The Merry Wives of Windsor

Much Ado About Nothing

As You Like It

King Henry V

Julius Caesar

Hamlet

Twelfth Night

Troilus and Cressida

All's Well That Ends Well

Measure for Measure

Othello

King Lear

Timon of Athens

Macbeth

Antony and Cleopatra

Pericles

Coriolanus

Cymbeline

The Winter's Tale

The Tempest

Two Noble Kinsmen (probably coauthored)

What Did Shakespeare Write About and Why?

Shakespeare's subjects include history, politics, magic, love of all kinds, religion, seafaring and exploration of new worlds, death, madness, ambition—in short, they reflect what concerned people both in their personal lives and in the country at large. It's tempting to theorize that Shakespeare had personal experience in everything he wrote about: If he wrote with authority on war, some have reasoned, he must have been in the military. But since we have no evidence that Shakespeare served as a soldier, worked as a gardener, went to sea, or clerked in a legal office, it's safer to assume that he was chiefly interested in writing a good play that audiences would enjoy. Since audiences were diverse, he had to be knowledgeable and clever about a wide range of subjects.

England in the sixteenth century was a small country rife with conflict and in the midst of change. New worlds were being discovered; the astronomer Copernicus's theory that the earth revolved around the sun had been proven correct. England fought a war with Spain, and the country worried about who would succeed the long-ruling Queen Elizabeth, as she had no heir. Internally, England's own people were divided by religion. Anglicans were at odds with Puritans, who wanted to strip away what they considered to be unnecessary Christian symbolism and excess in both religious and secular life. (In the early seventeenth century, Puritans managed to close down all the theaters in London.)

The countryside changed as well. Large areas of forest were cut down and turned into farms, while many rural people moved from farms and market towns such as Stratford into London and other cities. Finance, trade, and government expanded in the cities, as did poverty, overcrowding, and disease. City people and country folk, rich and poor, ignorant and learned, people of vast influence and those whose chief concern was getting a bit of bread each day—all are represented somewhere in Shakespeare's work.

Shakespeare's Audience

Shakespeare was intensely aware of his audience, and perhaps more than any other playwright, he wrote for the people who watched his plays. Music, dance, humor, and bawdy scenes were all incorporated to please royals, commoners, and everyone in between. Queen Elizabeth I loved plays and commissioned performances at her court. Admirals also provided support for plays by Shakespeare and other playwrights of the time, some of whom were rivals of Shakespeare's as well as friends. But these Anglican supporters were at odds with the Lord Mayor of London and the city's aldermen, who opposed theater and many other forms of entertainment. They regularly tried to close down theaters in the city, but their influence stopped at the city gates.

Shakespeare certainly depended on the support of the queen, but he relied just as much on playgoers from every other walk of life. Imagine a life without any modern forms of transportation to take us away, without any of the many ways in which we bring the larger world into our homes, and you will have some idea of how important live theater was to the Elizabethans. Londoners rich and poor were passionate about it, with thousands gathering for one performance. For a penny, viewers could stand in the central yard of the theater and watch the play; theater courtyards open to the afternoon sky were generally full of such "groundlings," regardless of the weather. Two pennies earned you a seat in the gallery, and various rooms and balconies overlooking the stage were reserved for wealthier playgoers.

Audience members at all levels used their imaginations freely to enhance their enjoyment of the plays. No one was bothered by boys playing women's roles, for example. (Women did not appear on the English stage during Shakespeare's time.) Suspending their sense of reality was both necessary and part of the fun for Shakespeare's contemporaries.

Theater Space

If you make a Shakespeare pilgrimage to England, you will find a reconstruction of the Globe Theatre on the same site where the original stood, in an outlying section of London. The Globe was only one of the theaters Shakespeare's plays were performed in, but with its characteristic oak timbers and thatched roof, it is surely the one most familiar to us. It was built in 1597 after an earlier theater used by Lord Chamberlain's Men was forced to close.

Even before proper theaters were built, plays were performed in inns and taverns. These simple spaces had far more in common with our school gyms or church basements than with professional theaters. They lacked any of the amenities we associate with modern theater, and playwrights kept the fancy devices to a minimum. There was no curtain, for example: Instead of a curtain coming down to signal the end of a scene, playwrights wrote into their scripts reasons for actors to leave the stage. A screen might close off one part of the stage allowing it to serve as a tomb or an inner sanctum of any kind. If there was a balcony over the inn courtyard, it was used for Juliet to lean over and talk to Romeo, or it could serve as a ship's deck or a castle window. There was often a trap door in the stage floor from which otherworldly creatures could emerge. Lights and sound systems were, of course, nonexistent, and there were virtually no sets.

What They Wore

The most valuable property owned by a theater company was its wardrobe, and Elizabethan audiences expected to see actors dressed in extravagant and elegant costumes with jewelry, silks, shoes, and gloves. Male characters carried swords when their roles called for them to do so. Audiences didn't much care if costumes were historically accurate, and costumes generally represented contemporary dress. Of course, there are plenty of poor and modestly dressed characters in Shakespeare, and these were easier and cheaper to outfit.

Speaking the Speech

For modern audiences young or old, seeing a play by Shakespeare can be a daunting experience because of the language. We often feel like we didn't quite catch what that character just said. Reading a play for the first time is even harder because we don't have the action in front of us, helping us piece together the playwright's intended meaning.

Some people are less bothered by not understanding right away. Some children, especially, just watch the action of a play and enjoy it, particularly when things are lively—sword fighting, witches cackling over a mysterious brew, a handsome young guy singing songs to his lady friend, and so on. But others just can't get past the unfamiliar words; they simply must figure them out before they can go on.

For children, pretending to be the characters and saying their words aloud is the best way to discover the meaning. It's important not to project our own adult difficulties with understanding on children when we're introducing them to Shakespeare. Many kids will just go with it—letting the odd words and phrases roll off their tongues because they want to get on with the action. I've observed that kids like to say "thee" and "thou" and even "prithee" and "wherefore," especially if they're dressed as a king, a lady, or a knight. In both the original plays and my adapted ones, a surprising number of words or phrases can be explained in the context of what's going on.

What makes Shakespeare's language so tricky for us? Several things. The first is the most obvious: He used words we don't use anymore. Elizabethan audiences knew what "wherefore" and "anon" meant, but we no longer use those words to mean "why" and "soon." It's a good idea for the director to have a copy of the unabridged play handy so that the notes or glossary can be consulted. Most editors of Shakespeare's works are extremely conscientious about defining unfamiliar words.

Shakespeare also used different sentence constructions. He reversed the order of phrases or separated words we might put together. Titania says, "Out of this wood do not desire to go," where we would say, "Do not try to leave these woods." But Titania's way of saying it nicely rhymes with the next line: "Thou shalt remain here whether thou wilt or no" (*A Midsummer Night's Dream*, Act III, Scene 1).

Sometimes we have to read through a long sentence and hold the meaning of the first part in our head until we get to the end. Meanwhile, in the middle of the sentence, some other important information might be conveyed. Consider these first lines of *Romeo and Juliet*, spoken by the Chorus:

Two households, both alike in dignity,
In fair Verona where we lay our scene,
From ancient grudge break to new mutiny.

What Shakespeare is saying is that two prominent families who have long been rivals now have a new grudge. But in the middle of that sentence, we also learn that the play takes place in the city of Verona. It may not be a straightforward construction, but from the writer's point of view, it is an efficient way to convey information.

Shakespeare had a tendency to omit words he considered unnecessary, especially in informal dialogue, but we do this in modern speech as well. We might say, "Going somewhere?" instead of "Are you going somewhere?" In *Twelfth Night*, Sebastian says, "Why I your purse?" to Antonio instead of "Why are you giving me your purse?" (Act III, Scene 3).

There is no doubt that Shakespeare's language can baffle us, but there are many times when his directness is striking and fresh. Consider these lines of Lysander to Demetrius (his rival for the love of Hermia) in the opening scene of *A Midsummer Night's Dream*:

You have her father's love, Demetrius.
Let me have Hermia's. Do you marry him.

It's not necessary to italicize the word *him* to understand Lysander's scorn.

Whether we are reading, watching, or performing Shakespeare, our own language is enriched. During the past four hundred years, the English language has assumed countless phrases and words from his work. Bartlett's *Familiar Quotations* has over 125 pages of them, and many of the sayings are so ingrained in our speech, we might have no idea they come from Shakespeare. Hamlet says, "What a piece of work is a man!" (Act III, Scene 2), and an echo sounds in our modern slang, "Man, he's a real piece of work!"

Bibliography

In most libraries and bookstores, you will find an array of interesting and beautiful books on Shakespeare written for children. Many of these are retellings of the most famous plays, singly or in collections. There are picture books for the very young and longer storybooks. Some are lavishly illustrated, some are serious, and some are meant to be humorous. You can also find books about Shakespeare himself and about the Elizabethan period that are intended for children.

Of course, you will want to consult unabridged editions of Shakespeare's plays, as well as nonfiction works that deal with the playwright and his life and times. In writing my adaptations, I consulted numerous editions, but two paperback series were the most helpful: the Folger Shakespeare Library editions and the Pelican Shakespeare editions. Within these series, each play is available separately, edited by a different Shakespeare scholar, and includes notes and introductory material. There are many other editions of the plays.

In addition to consulting books, type "Shakespeare" or "Shakespeare for children" into your Web browser, and many thousands of sites will come up. You can find everything from maps to lesson plans to pronunciation guides to links for youth theater programs on the Internet. Books are there too.

The list below reflects some of the books I have found, liked, and consulted. There are many others. I offer it only as a representative sampling of the range of books available.

Chrisp, Peter. *Shakespeare.* (New York: Dorling Kindersley, 2004).

Chute, Marchette. *Shakespeare of London.* (New York: EP Dutton, 1949.)

———. *An Introduction to Shakespeare.* (New York: EP Dutton,1951.)

Coville, Bruce. *William Shakespeare's Hamlet* (New York: Dial, 2004.) A prose retelling of the original play.

———. *William Shakespeare's Macbeth* (New York: Dial, 1997.) A prose retelling of the original play.

———. *William Shakespeare's A Midsummer Night's Dream* (New York: Dial, 1996.) A prose retelling of the original play.

———. *William Shakespeare's Romeo and Juliet* (New York: Dial, 1999.) A prose retelling of the original play.

———. *William Shakespeare's The Tempest* (New York: Philomel, 1996.) A prose retelling of the original play.

———. *William Shakespeare's Twelfth Night* (New York: Dial, 2003.) A prose retelling of the original play.

Davidson, Rebecca Piatt. *All the World's a Stage.* (New York: Greenwillow, 2003.)

Garfield, Leon. *Shakespeare Stories.* (Boston: Houghton Mifflin, 1985.)

———. *Shakespeare Stories II.* (Boston: Houghton Mifflin, 1995.)

Greenblatt , Stephen. *Will in the World: How Shakespeare Became Shakespeare* (New York: W.W. Norton, 2004.) For adults or older students.

Lamb, Charles and Mary. *Tales from Shakespeare.* (London: Penguin, 1994.) (First published 1807.)

Mayer, Marianna. *William Shakespeare's The Tempest.* (San Francisco: Chronicle Books, 2005.)

Mayhew, James (illustrator). *To Sleep, Perchance to Dream: A Child's Book of Rhymes.* (New York: Chickenhouse/Scholastic, 2001.)

Mowat, Barbara A. and Paul Werstine, editors. *Folger Shakespeare Library series.* (New York: Washington Square Press, 1992–2004.)

Packer, Tina. *Tales from Shakespeare.* (New York: Scholastic, 2004.)

The Pelican Shakespeare Series. (New York: Penguin, 1992–2002.)

Ross, Stewart. *Shakespeare and Macbeth: The Story Behind the Play.* (New York: Viking, 1994.)

Rubie, Peter. *The Everything Shakespeare Book: A Comprehensive Guide to Understanding the Comedies, Tragedies, and Sonnets of the Bard.* (Holbrook, Mass.: Adams Media, 2002.) For adults or older students.

Shapiro, James. *A Year in the Life of William Shakespeare: 1599.* (New York: HarperCollins, 2006.) For adults or older students.

Williams, Marcia. *Bravo, Mr. William Shakespeare.* (Cambridge, Mass.: Candlewick Press, 2000.)

Appendix C

Sample Letter Home

Teachers: As simple as your production is going to be, you can always use help. Many parents are willing to help assemble costume pieces or paint scenery, as long as you are clear about what you need. Adapt this letter for your own needs and send it home early in the rehearsal process.

Dear Parents and Guardians:

As your child may have already mentioned, we're starting our English [Reading/Language Arts] unit on the playwright William Shakespeare. During class time we have already read [book title] and [book title] about Shakespeare, and we've discussed the time in which he lived. The students are very excited about what will be the culmination of this unit: a production of [title of play] on [date of performance].

This play will be about forty minutes long. It will be great fun to rehearse and perform, but please understand that we are *not* aiming for professional quality! We will be using class time for rehearsals and for the performance. Of course, we would love it if parents, grandparents, and at-home siblings are able to attend, but attendance is optional and we do not want you to feel bad if you can't leave work to be there. This is mainly for the students and their student audience.

We appreciate any help you might be able to give in time or materials. No, you will not be required to go out and buy (or stay home and sew!) a fancy costume for your child to wear. Props, scenery, and costumes will be kept as simple as possible. A short list of costume and prop items we're looking for follows and a sheet is attached describing the costume your own child will wear. Most of the items are easy to find: a nightgown or a synthetic silky blouse, some old pants or leggings, a belt. Just a few, such as masks or plastic daggers, are a little harder. Please help us gather the costume items your own child will need. [If necessary, give a date by which costume must be complete and in school. This can be in a separate note home.]

If you have some extra time, we would love your help painting scenery. We will be meeting on the following days: [dates, times]. Grandparents and older brothers or sisters are also welcome to help.

As always, thanks for your support.

Yours truly,

SMITH AND KRAUS
PLAYS FOR GRADES K–6

10-MINUTE PLAYS

10-Minute Plays Volume IV for Kids/10+ Format Comedy by Kristen Dabrowski isbn 978-1-57525-441-8 $16.95 pp: 240

10-Minute Plays Volume V for Kids/10+ Format Drama by Kristen Dabrowski isbn 978-1-57525-438-8 $16.95 pp: 240

WORLD CULTURE PLAYS

Multicultural Plays for Children Grades K–3 by Pamela Gerke isbn 978-1-57525-005-2 $19.95 pp: 161

Multicultural Plays for Children Grades 4–6 by Pamela Gerke isbn 978-1-57525-006-9 $19.95 pp: 194

Fairy Tales, Grades K–3 by L.E. McCullough isbn 978-1-57525-109-7 $14.95 pp: 2183

Mythology, Grades 4–6 by L. E. McCullough isbn 978-1-57525-110-3 $14.95 pp: 141

People at Work, Grades K–3 by L. E. McCullough isbn 978-1-57525-140-0 $14.95 pp: 156

EDUCATIONAL SKITS

"Now I Get It!" Grades K–3 36 Ten-Minute Skits about Science, Math, Language, and Social Studies for Fun and Learning by L. E. McCullough isbn 978-1-57525-161-5 $16.95 pp: 136

"Now I Get It!" Grades 4–6 36 Ten-Minute Skits about Science, Math, Language, and Social Studies for Fun and Learning by L. E. McCullough isbn 978-1-57525-162-2 $16.95 pp: 141

JUDEO/CHRISTIAN HERITAGE PLAYS

Ancient Israel, Grades K–3 by L. E. McCullough isbn 978-1-57525-252-0 $15.95 pp: 163

Israel Reborn, Grades 4–6 by L. E. McCullough isbn 1978-1-57525-253-7 $15.95 pp: 204

Plays of the Songs of Christmas by L. E. McCullough isbn 978-1-57525-062-5 $19.95 pp: 131

(8 1/2 X 11) plays include: *Here We Come A-Wassailing; Silent Night; The Twelve Days of Christmas; O, Christmas Tree; Diamonds in the Snow; Jingle Bells; Good King Wenceslas; O Thou Joyful Day; Let Us Go, O Shepherds; Bring a Torch, Jeannette, Isabella; We Three Kings of Orient Are; Go Tell It on the Mountain*

AMERICAN HISTORY PLAYS

America from American Folklore, Grades K–6 by L. E. McCullough isbn 978-1-57525-038-0 $14.95 pp: 161

Wild West, Grades K–3 by L. E. McCullough isbn 978-1-57525-104-2 $14.95 pp: 150

Wild West, Grades 4–6 by L. E. McCullough isbn 978-1-57525-105-9 $14.95 pp: 196

WORLD HISTORY PLAYS

Exploration and Discovery, Grades 4–6 by L. E. McCullough isbn 978-1-57525-113-4 $14.95 pp: 157

To order books or request a free annual catalogue
call toll-free (888) 282-2881 or visit www.smithandkraus.com.